I0825458

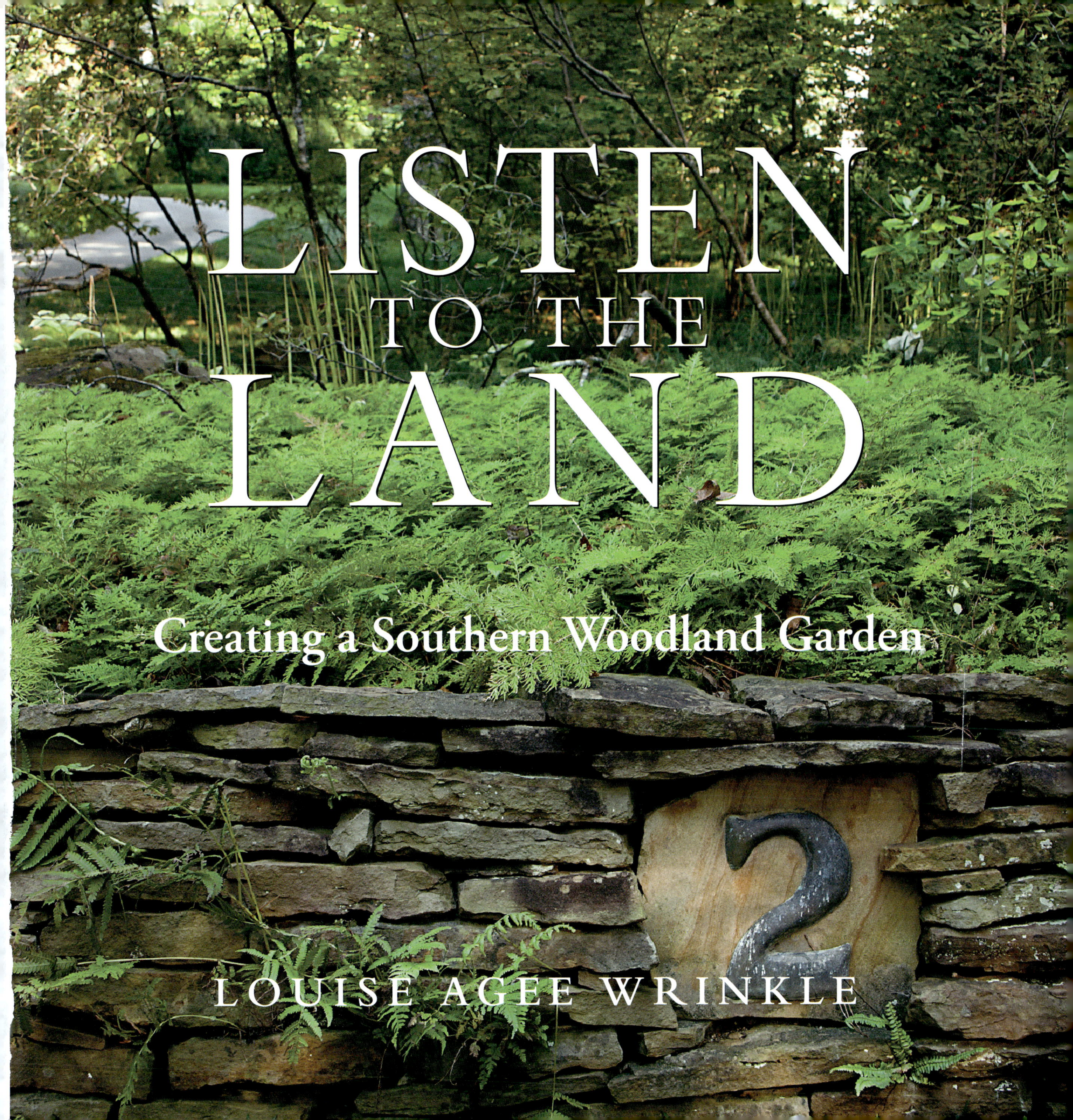
LISTEN
TO THE
LAND
Creating a Southern Woodland Garden
2
LOUISE AGEE WRINKLE

# LISTEN TO THE LAND

## Creating a Southern Woodland Garden


LOUISE AGEE WRINKLE

PHOTOGRAPHY BY
Mick Hales
Sylvia Martin
Norman Kent Johnson
Beth Maynor Young
Margaret Wrinkle
Louise Wrinkle

UPDATED WITH A NEW PREFACE BY
James Brayton Hall
President and CEO, The Garden Conservancy

FOREWORDS BY
John Alex Floyd, Jr., Ph.D.
Retired Vice President and Editor-in-Chief, *Southern Living*

Fred Spicer
Executive Vice President and Director, Chicago Botanic Garden

DESIGN BOOKS

For Margaret and Anne


Printed in the United States of America through
Porter Print Group, Bethesda, Maryland

ISBN: 979-8-9896026-0-5
Library of Congress Number available on request

Photographs © Mick Hales; Sylvia Martin; Norman Kent Johnson; Beth Maynor Young; Margaret Wrinkle; Louise Wrinkle. Map illustration © John Wilson, Golightly Landscape Architecture

Author photo © Irene Gardner

louisewrinkle.com

Editor: Cathy Still McGowin
Designer: Rebecca Reeves
Editorial Assistant: Molly C. Lipski



First published in 2017 by Birmingham Home and Garden; updated edition published in 2024 by Design Books, Sharon, CT.

Design Books are distributed by
National Book Network
15200 NBN Way
Blue Ridge Summit, PA 17214
(717) 794-3800
Customercare@nbnbooks.com

Special thanks to The Garden Conservancy for its generous support of this edition of *Listen to the Land*, and to James Brayton Hall for his new preface. The book has been reissued to coincide with the launch of The Garden Conservancy's documentary film on Louise Agee Wrinkle and her garden.

***There is just as much beauty visible to us in the landscape as we are prepared to appreciate, not a grain more.***

• Henry David Thoreau, *Excursions* •

# CONTENTS

# PREFACE

I have always believed that in all the best ways, *a garden is a conversation*. First and foremost, it is a conversation between the site, the gardener, and the plants. It might also include the designer, the neighbors, visitors and friends, and other gardeners looking for inspiration.

Louise Wrinkle's garden exemplifies all the best of these dialogues. This land has been calling to Louise for a very long time. She heard its voice as a horse-crazy young girl when it was simply "the Jungle." Those of us who have read this book or had the privilege of visiting Louise's remarkable garden in person can see the wonderful result of her long and fruitful conversations with the land where she grew up.

Garden talk rarely remains in the garden. Like certain plants, it has a tendency to self-sow. It is one of The Garden Conservancy's missions to spark and continue these rich conversations down through and across the generations. As a founding board member of The Garden Conservancy in 1989, Louise, along with her friend Leigh Allison, participated in one of its first continuing national events designed to foster these conversations by directing Open Days in Birmingham for several years, opening her garden to the public then as she has often.

Mountain Brook, Alabama, is a beautiful, verdant community rich with remarkable gardens in a broad diversity of styles, thanks to the original planners, Olmstead and Manning, who recognized and protected the unspoiled natural beauty of its woods, streams, and mountains. When I was first invited by my friend Camille Butrus to visit Mountain Brook's best gardens, the breadth of the conversations inspired by Louise's garden was evident. No other garden was like the Wrinkle garden, but each proud homeowner said to me quite casually, "Well, of course when I was thinking about putting in a garden, before I did anything I asked Louise to come over and tell me what she thought." It was always about *listening* . . .

On that first visit, I listened as well. Every gardener asked me the same question: "What will become of Louise's garden?" Louise's response to that concern was to write this book, which records her 30-year adventure of listening to and working with this land where she grew up rather than imposing a personal design upon it. The Garden Conservancy's response has been to make a documentary film about Louise, her garden, and her powerful influence on fellow gardeners and designers. Thanks to Suzanne Rheinstein's vision of adding a video element to our garden documentation process, we have begun to capture the living, breathing essence of each important landscape in our work. However, Louise is our only garden creator still alive to talk about her influences and decisions. The documentary about Louise and her garden will premiere on the occasion of Birmingham's Open Days relaunch in May 2024.

Our numerous visits and interviews with many gardeners Louise has inspired have in turn led to the publication of a second edition of *Listen to the Land*. (The first edition sold out.) This book offers an appropriate and timely opportunity for all gardeners, environmentalists, native plant enthusiasts, and just plain lovers of beauty to sharpen their thoughts about how a garden can grow beyond just wonderful horticulture. Listen not only to the land but also to Louise, as she describes a lifelong love affair and thoughtful conversations with a very special place.

James Brayton Hall
President and CEO,
The Garden Conservancy

# FOREWORD

***Listen to the Land* articulates an understanding of garden evolution. Gardens evolve sometimes from things we gardeners do, sometimes from a change of focus, or sometimes and most often from Mother Nature.**

With every change—whether initiated by the gardener or imposed upon her by the weather—comes opportunity. Louise Wrinkle understands this better than most. In the 30 years since she started her Birmingham garden, she's always had the goal of creating a space that has been built with the land, not against it.

The first time I visited Louise's garden was the winter of 1987, when she and Beaty Hanna were having his crew install a hedge of beautiful hollies along the roadway for screening. A bit later I saw a straight-line drive to the house transformed into a perfect S-curved entrance through the garden. With nearly every visit to her house, I witnessed changes—some big, some small. Regardless of the evolution, the feeling remained the same—that I was entering a very special place that is a garden first, with the residence sitting in the middle of paradise.

One of the things Louise has done regarding building and evolving is to have a team of folks give her advice. Beaty Hanna and his team were instrumental in the early years. They helped install the garden and also had a keen eye for what would grow where and how to get the unique plant elements to work together horticulturally. Norman Johnson, who is still part of the team today, has been a constant voice, helping maintain the garden's elegant but subtle design. Louise and her team have built what I consider one of the most thoughtful and beautiful gardens in Birmingham by working with the landscape, allowing the natural beauty to show itself, and enhancing that beauty with thoughtful planning.

But this book is not limited just to inspired design. The Plant Profiles will be valuable to any gardener. This is a list of plants that Louise has had in her garden and her personal experience with each of them. I learned so much from this section, even though I actively garden at home as often as my schedule allows.

As you read this book, remember that the woman who says she went from "horses to horticulture" not only gave us a great garden but also is a realist who understands that as a garden evolves over time, new challenges and opportunities abound. This book reflects the ability of one woman to make her home and garden the perfect blend of nature and design.

—John Alex Floyd, Jr., Ph.D., retired Vice President and Editor-in-Chief, *Southern Living*

# FOREWORD

***This is a love story with a tenderness that's understated, unexpected, but entirely undeniable. To non-gardeners, this compulsion may seem a bit curious or misunderstood. Yet it is a deep fascination with the* genius loci*, the spirit of the place, and its responses to a caring and protective human hand.***

To know Birmingham, Alabama, as a place of stunning, personal, intimate, opulent, idiosyncratic, funky, and traditional gardens you either have to live there for a while, garden there for a while, or know some people who do both and visit them. If you do any of that, and have any interest at all in gardens and gardening, you will soon learn about Birmingham neighborhoods like Forest Park and Redmont, and its leafy suburb of Mountain Brook. And you'll likely meet some gardeners, too.

This is a book about a garden, written by a gardener who grew up in it, and later returned to remake it and grow it, as only a gardener can. It's a coming-of-age story that spans a lifetime and resolves with a sentimental quandary. It's also about the kinds of friends and talents you meet along the way—fellow enthusiasts, professional designers, and the local police.

This is also a book about the education of a gardener. It speaks to the frustrating persistence of trial and error, and the often anonymous, quiet satisfaction of a single, successful bloom. There are challenges to rise to: insects, stubborn soil, weeds, drought, flood, sun, frost, microburst, and tornadoes. There are practical conundrums (like where to store the Billy Goat) and surprising journeys to find the solutions.

Most of us will never create this kind of garden. But much of what this book speaks to is attainable by many, even though all of it as a whole may not be. In this way, the parts and insights are far more valuable than the sum.

The notion of garden design is compelling, but for gardeners it's really about the love of plants. It's the stories about who gave each plant to you, where you first saw them, how many times you've tried them—and even killed them—and how really, really right that one is in that particular spot (once you have figured that out).

I am fortunate to know this garden (and its plants and who built what) pretty well. I know the gardener, the author, Louise Agee Wrinkle, pretty well, too. I've been toured around her garden enough by her to lead tours. I watched it grow for fifteen years (really only briefly), and can even lay claim to having added a few plants to it, perhaps even in places I recommended they be planted. And I made a friend, too.

—Fred Spicer, Executive Vice President and Director, Chicago Botanic Garden

***To the attentive eye, each moment of the year has its own beauty, and in the same field, it beholds, every hour, a picture which was never seen before, and which shall never be seen again.***

• Ralph Waldo Emerson, *Nature* •

# INTRODUCTION

When people ask me the style of my garden, I reply, "It's a natural woodland." Should they ask further, I will admit to being a minimalist. I want only those things which would naturally appear in a woodland garden. I have a strong feeling that, as gardeners, we should let the land speak for itself rather than impose our own thoughts and preferences upon it.

At our family property on Beechwood Road in Mountain Brook, a suburb of Birmingham, Alabama, I have always preferred to listen rather than to dictate. By listening to this unspoiled piece of Alabama woodland, I've learned how to nurture and protect its unique character.

I keep hearing Thoreau's dictum: Simplify, simplify.

Mother always said, "Count your blessings." Often, I reflect on how lucky I am for having this property and the ability to care for it with no one to answer to but myself. I realize that the strength of my bond with this land most likely stems from the fact that I spent most of my childhood in this spot, with parents who taught me how to be in dialogue with my natural surroundings. Years later, after my parents died, I was fortunate enough to move back into my family home, taking over my mother's garden and making it my own.

Nestled between the foothills of the Appalachians as they transition into coastal plains, my garden contains rolling hills, gigantic trees, a running stream, and a variety of interesting plants. Flat land is intermittent at best. The paths lead from one level to the next, often with steps up or down, and the horizon is never in sight. There are few long vistas; instead there are surprises around every corner.

People often talk about *genius loci*, or the spirit of a place, but too often, they impose their own personal preferences and patterns on a piece of land, which can alter its inherent character and obliterate the natural dialogue of the place. Of course, some areas have more to say than others. My lifelong connection with this piece of Alabama woodland has taught me how to hear its particular voice.

I might not have been such a minimalist if I had had more training in landscape design. But if I'd had that training, I'd probably mess with things more than I've been inclined to do. I feel the less done the better. I prefer to let the land and its contours suggest plantings. We can have plant groupings and natural thickets, but I'm very much in favor of leaving space to breathe. In an appreciation of forest aesthetics, a certain amount of editing must be done to eliminate clutter and emphasize the grandeur around us, but God does pretty well when left alone or given only gentle assistance.

In contrast to many gardeners, I do not want to emulate any particular style: the sweeping greensward of a Capability Brown English Garden, the precisely-clipped hedges of a French parterre, nor the tall, dark, green cypress exclamation points of an Italian garden. Neither am I interested in creating garden rooms made famous at English gardens like Sissinghurst or Hidcote. I prefer to have the different areas flow into each other and maintain their relationships to the whole rather than to set each apart.

*Japanese roof iris* (Iris tectorum) *line the stream bank.*

One of the advantages of visiting other people's gardens is to gather ideas that you can take home and try. Countless gardeners go to the British Isles to be inspired by the gardens there, and, thankfully, plagiarism is alive and well in the gardening world. Many Americans think of English gardens as "a consummation devoutly to be wished." Then, after visiting, they want to come home and put their heads in the oven because they can't duplicate what they have just enjoyed.

Rarely do gardeners consider the location of the United Kingdom on the globe in relation to the sun. The British Isles lie between parallels 50 and 60, opposite from Newfoundland in North America. It is the unique juxtaposition of this northerly latitude protected by the warming Gulf Stream that offers the Brits the full northern sun and simultaneously cool temperatures for optimum plant growth of so many beautiful flowering perennials, shrubs, and trees.

In contrast, Birmingham, Alabama, lies much further south between parallels 34 and 35. We are gardening in a much more difficult environment here, where summer temperatures can reach 95-100 during the day without cooling much at night. High humidity may be good for the skin, but can be enervating to the gardener. Winter temperatures are fickle; we may bask in the 70s for days before dropping back into the 40s, or sometimes much lower, and we are allowed no snow cover to protect plants. These difficulties can teach you to focus on your own location or ignore it at your peril.

Any serious gardener is going to have visitors. When gardeners, designers, botanists, and horticulturists come here, I like to pick their educated brains with all the questions I have. When they arrive, I usually give them a map to make sure they will see everything I want to share with them. My visitors can look at the map and see where they are, where they have been, and what remains.

Attached to the map I hand out is a plant list, containing the botanical and common names of several hundred

LEFT AND OPPOSITE: *I learned to prune miniature cut-leaf Japanese maples* (Acer palmatum) *from the inside to reveal their graceful skeletons which become even more striking in winter.*

plants I have experimented with here. I started this practice after learning that Christopher Lloyd, the famous English writer, plantsman, and owner of Great Dixter, complained that people would ask, "What is that plant?" and he would tell them, then would have to spell it out. He thought it simpler to provide a list.

I've also included a section in this book called "Plant Profiles," based on the plant list, but containing annotations of my experiences with these plants—those that succeeded and those that failed. It is my hope that gardeners may benefit from understanding what worked and what didn't work for me, how different areas have been developed, and how time and age have affected this place.

I had made stabs at writing about what this garden is and how it came to be, but the pages never materialized into anything. It wasn't until I received an email from well-known garden photographer Mick Hales that I was prompted to move forward. Mick had visited several years before on an assignment to photograph gardens of members of The Garden Club of America for *Gardens Private & Personal*. Now he asked if I would be interested in writing a book on my garden. I commissioned him to photograph in fall and spring. Some of the best images herein were taken by Mick.

When I first tried to organize my thoughts, I was torn between basing my record on geography or chronology, that is, concentrating on different areas we worked on or when we worked on them. It occurred to me that I could treat the reader as my garden visitor. Creating a written tour would allow me to describe the different areas we have developed, how they have evolved or remained the same, and how I react to them.

We all know that gardens reflect the owner's personality. In one of my garden books, I ran across a quote to the effect that the footprint of the owner is worth more than a load of manure, meaning that the owner must shoulder the responsibility of actually managing the property and not leave the demanding work to anyone (or anything) else. I was astonished to learn that the quote came from Lyndon B. Johnson, whom I had not thought of as a gardener or a naturalist. Another thought along the same vein is the Arab saying: "The eye of the master makes the horse grow fat." In other

BELOW: *My favorite natural sculpture is a mature Hawthorn* (Craetaegus spathulata). *Probably more than 100 years old, this tree has been here longer than my family has. It is now the centerpiece of one area of my garden.*

RIGHT: *Given to me by Frank Cabot, this Katsura tree* (Cercidiphyllum japonicum) *frames one view of the path looking towards the Wooden Bridge.*

OPPOSITE: *Mature Piedmont azaleas* (Rhododendron canescens) *can grow 12-15 feet and perfume the whole area.*

words, by nurturing and strengthening the connection between ourselves and the land surrounding us, we open our ears to hear all that it has to say.

Most serious gardeners are truly enlightened when it comes to protecting and improving the land, just as serious hunters are known to be conservationists of the highest order. General Eisenhower was the first I knew to say that he wanted to look to the future in order to leave the land better than he found it. His thought reminds me of those English gardeners who plant trees for their grandchildren to enjoy.

These days we seem to be spoiled, always demanding instant gratification. Even when we can wait for a moment, the focus still seems to be on

*Mature Piedmont azaleas* (Rhododendron canescens) *can grow 12-15 feet and perfume the whole area.*

the short term. We look for tomorrow, next month, next year, instead of for coming generations. Our culture has been built upon consuming precious resources; we mine ore, pump oil, cut trees, fish the oceans. In the South, we are fortunate to be able to timber every fifteen years, but other areas do not have such a long growing season to produce a renewable crop. Commercial activity lasts only as long as the resource remains or can be replenished. The lumber mills work only while there are trees available to cut; irresponsible over-fishing of our oceans has forced us to farm them artificially after we have decimated the natural supply. I sincerely hope we never reach the point described in the Native American truth: "Only when the last tree has died and the last river been poisoned and the last fish been caught will we realize we cannot eat money."

We must look to the long term in order to leave something for our grandchildren's tomorrows—something far more valuable than discarded digital gadgets, gas-guzzling vehicles, and abandoned shopping malls. When we rely on good gardeners everywhere to take a message of responsible ownership to the world at large, while protecting and preserving our own few acres of land, we become the careful stewards of our common bounty.

These pages represent a record of my simple yet determined efforts to do that by creating a natural garden in an unspoiled Alabama woodland.

# FEATURES:

1. Driveway
2. Berm
3. Sea of mondo grass
4. Entrance Court
5. Fountain
6. Belgian Fence
7. Sunken Garden
8. Three Stone Bench
9. Cutting Garden
10. Potting Shed
11. St. Fiacre
12. Bamboo Arch
13. Brook
14. Wooden Bridge
15. Spencer's Bench
16. Stone Bridge
17. New Bridge
18. Pond
19. Gate
20. Woodhill Steps
21. Stone Bench
22. Tornado Alley/Meadow
23. Stone Circle
24. Millstone Fountain

# PLANTS NOTED:

A. Native azaleas *(Rhododendron canescens)*
B. Tulip Poplar *(Liriodendron tulipifera)*
C. Beech *(Fagus grandifolia)*
D. Stewartia *(Stewartia koreana)*
E. Water Oak "Weed Trees," *(Quercus nigra)*
F. Clutch of Farkleberries *(Vaccinium arboreum)*
G. Chinese quince *(Pseudocydonia sinensis)*
H. Hemlocks *(Tsuga canadensis)*
I. Winter Daphne *(Daphne ordora 'Aureomarginata')*
J. Hawthorn *(Crataegus spathulata)*
K. Evergreen Dogwood *(Cornus capitata)*
L. Parrotia *(Parrotia persica)*
M. Winter Hazel *(Corylopsis glabrescens)*
N. Six Dwarfs *(Ilex x 'Emily Brunner')*

Map includes topographic contour lines indicating rise and fall of hills and valleys.

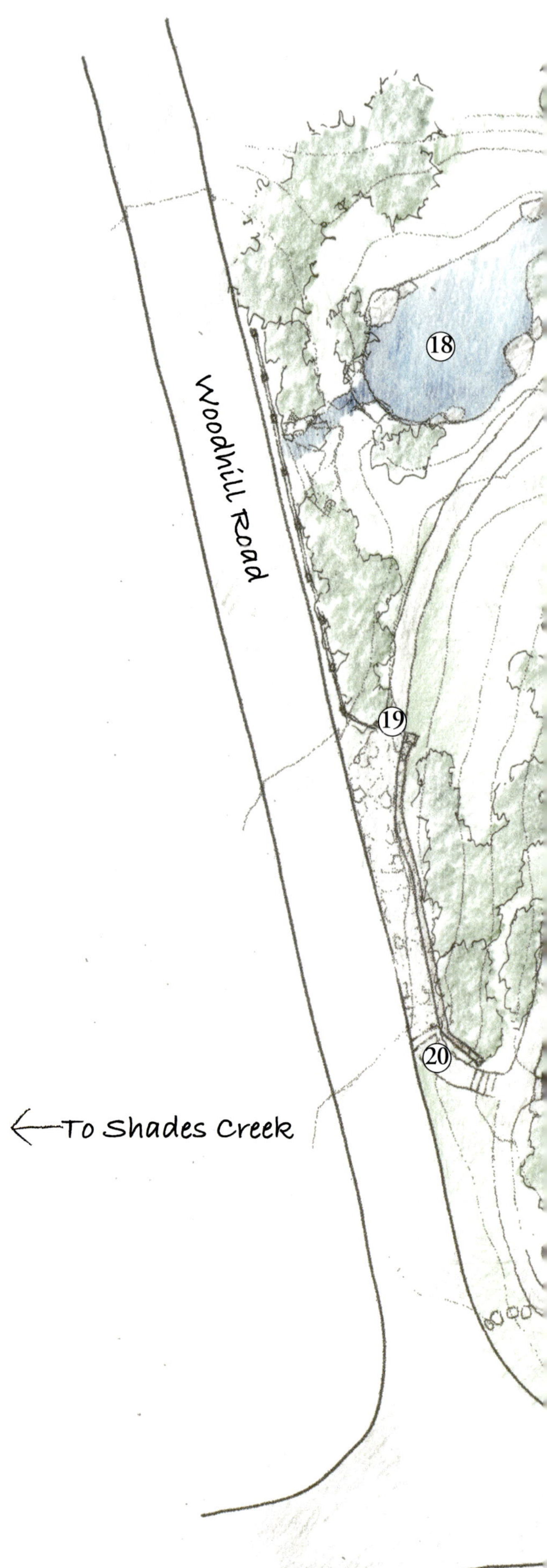

Driveway
Beechwood Road
N

***Just as the twig is bent, the tree's inclined.***

• Alexander Pope, *Moral Essays* •

# 1

# WE CALLED IT THE JUNGLE

I first saw the property that would become my home at 2 Beechwood Road from the back of a rented pony in 1938 when I was just six years old. I began to ride at Mountain Brook Riding Academy, on what was then the outskirts of Birmingham, Alabama. My memory of lessons is hazy, but as soon as we learned to post the trot and sit the canter, we were allowed to ride out with Mother's friend Mrs. Headley, in her snap brim fedora. On Sunday afternoons, she led a group of 10 or 12 youngsters on a bridle trail laid out in Robert Jemison's original 1920s development of Mountain Brook, a beautiful suburb of Birmingham, featuring tree-covered hills, valleys, and streams. The trail was about 12 miles long, following Watkins Brook and Shades Creek to the Mountain Brook Club golf course. At the Club, we would often leave our horses in the corral and go inside for a Coke or a glass of iced tea before riding back to the stable.

The property we passed before arriving at the Club was known to us riders as The Jungle because it was overgrown with honeysuckle, poison ivy, and weed trees. It was impenetrable. When I learned that my parents had bought a little over two acres of property adjacent to that particular place to build their first house, I told them our name for it. The Jungle has become my garden.

Birmingham was a new city, founded in 1871 to exploit the proximity of coal, iron ore, and limestone needed to make iron and steel. While the city was rising, a young visionary developer named Robert Jemison, Jr., was designing the ancillary neighborhoods of Forest Park and Redmont to accommodate the city's growing population. He also developed the neighboring town of Fairfield to house the people involved with the steel mills. In these successful endeavors, he had enlisted landscape architect Warren Manning, who had begun his career in the Boston office of Frederick Law Olmstead and who was already famous for designing New York's Central Park. The next wave of Jemison's and Manning's developments was Mountain Brook. This new neighborhood was dubbed Over the Mountain because it lay on the far side of a mass of iron ore named Red Mountain. After his review of this new territory, Manning reported to Jemison that the land was "wild and picturesque," and he advised the use of "indigenous landscape." From the beginning, Mountain Brook was seen in the eyes of land planners as a place of great natural beauty to protect and maintain.

When we built our house, the effects of the Great Depression were still acutely felt. There was very little residential work, so quality builders were readily available and construction progressed quickly. Our house was only the second on the street. Trees had to be cleared, but they were carefully selected to accommodate the house and drive only. Dogwoods, pines, tulip poplars, Southern magnolias, and other Southern woodland species covered the rest of the property.

Money was tight and Daddy wanted no frills. We moved into the house in June 1938, and every effort was made to make it comfortable but thrifty.

*At six years old, I was a budding equestrian who told my parents the new property they had bought on Beechwood Road was called "The Jungle."*

There was virtually no molding inside (that was to come in the early 1950s). To conserve space, the coat closet was built under the staircase, and to save on paving costs, the driveway went straight to the street. Still, the house was grand for its time: a traditional red brick two-story Georgian with the front door on the side and boxwood on the corners.

No houses had air conditioning, and the temperatures were the usual 85 to 95 degrees for Alabama summers. Like most houses, ours was equipped with a large attic fan. After dark, Mother would open windows downstairs and let the fan pull in the cooler night air. Early in the morning, she would close the windows and draperies to keep the house noticeably cooler.

In Southern tradition, Mother changed the rugs, draperies, and slipcovers to summer attire every May. Oriental rugs were rolled with newspaper as a cheap moth repellent and replaced with grass rugs. Heavy draperies were swapped with sheers, and lighter slipcovers offered a cooler look, particularly downstairs. Mother enlisted several strong backs to tote the winter trappings to the attic. The draperies were stored in a large coffin-

---

ABOVE: *Sketch by Hugh Martin, architect of Agee house on Beechwood Road with Mother's handwriting below: "Our house which was built in 1938 at 2 Beechwood Road. We moved in June 1st 1938." Coincidentally, my husband John and I moved into the new/old house in June 1988, exactly 50 years later.*

OPPOSITE: *A healthy spread of Snowdrops* (Leucojum vernum) *at the bottom of the driveway has expanded since Mother planted them years ago.*

ABOVE: *My sister, Kitty (left) and me, about 14 and 12 years old.*

LEFT: *A painting of my mother, Margaret Minge Agee.*

RIGHT: *My father, Rucker Agee.*

OPPOSITE: *As a housewarming present, my grandmother Minge had ordered an assortment of spring bulbs for the new yard, and my parents were to plant them. At first sight of a couple hundred daffodil bulbs, my father wondered: "Why so few?" After an afternoon or two of planting, he wondered: "Why so many?"*

like box. We no longer change the décor with the seasons, but that box remains, full of relics from the past.

We had no near neighbors, so we grew up basically undisturbed. The Jungle turned out to be the perfect place for my sister Kitty and me to immerse ourselves in a natural playground. Despite having a new house, Kitty, who was two years older, and I preferred to play in the woods and along nearby Shades Creek. We saw turtles and fish but relatively few snakes. From time to time, trees would fall across the creek and it took nerve and balance for us to cross from one side to the other.

We made frequent trips to a blackberry patch nearby. Picking the plump fruits involved stepping deep into the bushes which were loaded not only with berries but also with chiggers, or redbugs, a sure source of itching welts. My grandmother Agee used natural remedies, and she made sure our socks and the inside of our shoes were liberally dusted with flowers of sulfur, which repelled the chiggers and was easily washed off before we helped concoct a delicious cobbler at home.

One of the few times I do remember playing with other children was on my seventh birthday. It was not a particularly festive get-together, for the only guests were those who had survived that season's terrible whooping cough epidemic. A motley crew of about 12 hollow-eyed children appeared to mark the occasion. In those polio days, we were not allowed to visit crowded places like swimming pools or movie theatres.

Kitty and I roamed the developing neighborhood on foot and bicycles. A couple of miles down Shades Creek was the Old Mill, a tearoom built in the 1920s to lure prospective real estate clients into this new development. Nestled into the creek bank, it had a millwheel that turned at the opening of a lock in the dam. A bridge ran over the creek to the front door. After the tearoom closed during the Great Depression, Kitty and I, unbeknownst to our parents, spent hours clambering through and around the massive wooden wheel that could have cut us in two.

Kitty was popular, pretty, smart, and tended to be a leader, so much so that she insisted on that role. She was a good athlete, performing well at swimming, softball, and tennis, but unlike me, she didn't like horses, and in her letters from camp she begged to be released from the riding requirement. Like many siblings, the older one tends to be the authoritative one; close family and friends thought her domineering. I certainly did. As a child, she was always organizing clubs, provided she was the president. In contrast to Kitty's outstanding popularity, I just limped along as the overshadowed little sister, an introvert with few friends, content as a loner. Mother hoped I would turn into a late bloomer.

Fortunately, my parents' love of nature would help me find my place in this world. I remember that each year or so my parents spent time debating which trees were to come out to make room for others to develop. In the beginning of our time here, they spent hours and days deciding the fates of various trees. We had so many native dogwoods, my parents planned parties in the spring to enjoy the clouds of white. Even now, after losing many dogwoods to age and disease, the bright reflection from the white bracts on those remaining can wake me on an early April morning.

An investment banker by trade, my father was also an avid naturalist and an early environmentalist. During our summer trips to the Gulf Coast, he collected sea shells. There are still boxes with giant starfish and even a rare paper nautilus in the attic. Back home, he took us on walks and taught us the common names of trees: maples, hickories, oaks, and pines. In addition to being a nature lover, Daddy was a map collector. He realized maps are a recording of history and place, and he became recognized as an amateur historian. His collection of pre-colonial Southeastern United States maps is now housed at The Birmingham Public Library.

Daddy's confidence in nature has always been a reassuring guide for me. When the pine bark beetle devastated most of the loblolly pines during the 1970s and people grew anxious, Daddy said, "Don't worry, nature is a

LEFT: *When we explored the property as children, we discovered arrowheads. Much later, when we cleared and restored the Brook, we unearthed a large mortar and pestle.*

OPPOSITE: *The profusion of native dogwood* (Cornus florida) *when we first moved to Beechwood Road continues to create a dazzling display every spring.*

great healer," and I added, "If you give it a chance." Perhaps I acquired my laissez-faire philosophy of gardening from him.

My mother, Margaret Minge Agee, was a true lady, an outstanding beauty with impeccable taste, who could do anything that needed doing, but like many Southern ladies, she preferred others do it for her. Her particular talent was washing anything, from Scottie dogs to felt hats. She made things look easy. She was independent and thrifty, whether shopping for antiques to furnish the house or hard trading with Armenian rug merchants. Sometimes we thought her bossy, but it was because she wanted the best for us. She had what we think of as a Southern sensibility—an appreciation of the finer things, including gardening and flower arranging which was not limited to flowers, for they were seasonal and not available all year. Her arrangements of all-green cuttings were popular and long-lasting, and she was a master at weaving a variety of textures into a pleasing composition that welcomed visitors to our front hall.

*A log cabin from the 1938 National Boy Scout Jamboree was given to my father. He had it moved from the Municipal Auditorium in Birmingham to our property. We used it as a play house. Notice the small American holly tree* (Ilex opaca) *in foreground; it has since become a massive giant. The present Cutting Garden is where the cabin once stood.*

Well before I became at all interested in gardening, I asked Mother one year what she wanted for Christmas. She mentioned that she would love to have a Cryptomaria. I had never heard of such an animal and had no idea what it was. I had to say it to myself phonetically. I broke it down into "crypto" and "Mary," picturing in my mind a Greek sarcophagus and an image of the Virgin Mary. I had to rush and write it down before I forgot so I could order it for her as a gift.

Now I am familiar with the Latin names, and I recognize Cryptomaria as one of our treasured Oriental evergreens that grow to 60 feet with branches covered in small, soft, needle-like leaves. Mother was delighted with the new shrub and planted it outside the Stone Circle, where it lasted until the Blizzard of 1993. By that time, my husband John and I were living back on Beechwood Road. After the storm, I noticed the towering evergreen had turned a brownish-purple color, and I thought it had died—burned from reflected light of the sun on the snow. So, I had it cut down, only to learn later that Cryptomaria often turns this color in winter. I still regret misreading its seasonal color for death.

While my parents were concentrating on making their house a home, Kitty and I continued to enjoy our Jungle playground and my father contributed the perfect new clubhouse for us. He was active with the Boy Scouts, even though he only had daughters. Every four years, the scouts held a National Jamboree. In the late 1930s, it was held in Birmingham. As part of the celebration, a simple log cabin was constructed on the floor of the municipal auditorium. When the festivities concluded, the scouts gave the cabin to Daddy. We were thrilled when he had it reassembled on the north side of the house up the hill from the Parking Court.

Our new one-room cabin was about 14 feet square. There was no heat, plumbing, or electricity, but it had two windows and a fireplace and we thought it quite special. There, we learned how to manage kerosene lanterns. The trick was the length of the wick, which, when burning, provided the light. If it was too long, it produced smoke and blackened the glass, which then had to be cleaned; if too short, the light diminished and even went out. The log cabin was where we kept our treasure trove of Big Little Books, which we enjoyed reading and rereading. They were a combination of text and pictures, printed in a chunky, thick, 4-inch-square book. As an added attraction, each page had a small picture in the upper corner. When the pages were flipped, the images became animated, much like a cartoon.

We had spend-the-night parties in the cabin, and Mother would leave the garage lights on and the side door of the house unlocked for anyone feeling cold or spooked during the night. As Kitty and I grew older, we used the hideaway to experiment with smoking the silvery leaves of rabbit tobacco growing outside, and occasionally a real cigarette. But the chinks did not absolutely fill the spaces between the logs. Often, we feared that the smoke would escape and we would be discovered by Marshall, Mother's right-hand man. We were more afraid of Marshall's strict discipline than even Mother's. He wouldn't say much, but his displeasure would be evident.

Marshall was a short, stocky, African-American man of mature years. He never moved quickly, but he did everything that Mother couldn't or didn't want to do: yard work, serving meals, heavy housework, and driving us when needed. Marshall took responsibility for many areas of concern including looking after the yard and the dog, a cocker spaniel named Blondie, who looked innocent but was known to bite. Marshall trained the dog not to enter the living room, which was reserved for company, and where to do her business down in the woods.

When any of us happened to run into snakes, Mother always said that they were more afraid of us than we were of them. She cautioned Marshall to kill only the venomous ones, but he claimed that every one of them was a water moccasin and did away with all the snakes he came across.

As we grew, so did the neighborhood. To support the population influx, Mountain Brook Elementary School had opened in 1929. While we grew up surrounded by woods and streams, the rest of the world endured the turmoil of World War II. In our protected Jungle, we were only inconvenienced with rationing of gasoline, shoes, butter, and sugar.

---

TOP: *This photo shows the driveway when it ran perpendicular to the street.*

ABOVE: *The living room at 2 Beechwood Road looks much the same as when my parents lived here.*

***In gardening, there is only one absolute rule: you have to garden where you are, not someplace else.***

• Allen Lacy, *The Garden in Autumn* •

# 2

# FROM HORSES TO HORTICULTURE

I never set out to be a plant nut. In college, I was more interested in zoology than botany, and then family filled my life. I married my husband, John Wrinkle, when I was 26, and we had two daughters, Anne and Margaret. When the girls were still small, I realized my childhood dream of owning my own horse, and luckily, the girls shared my passion.

Our first house had little more than a flat postage stamp of a lawn. The backyard contained an even smaller lawn and was enclosed by a privet hedge, an ivy-covered wall, and the building that contained the guest house and garage. It was a perfect place to look after children because they couldn't get loose and go anywhere. The small, flat yard was just enough for my husband to mow, but he always waited until 11 o'clock on a weekend morning to attack the small, green patch, and he inevitably developed a sweaty, red face. Each time I watched him gulp down a cold Coke in just a few swallows, I felt relief that he didn't have a stroke or heart attack. Obviously, my future love of gardening wouldn't be an interest we shared.

When the girls turned school age, we moved to Heathermoor Road, just up the hill from Mountain Brook Elementary School, my alma mater. I had entered the second grade there when it was a county school and graduated from its eighth grade in 1944. We lived on Heathermoor Road for 18 years, from 1968 to 1987, enjoying a large adjoining wooded lot that provided protection from neighbors and space for wildflowers. Once again, we had only a few (thankfully small) grassy areas which were easily maintained with our old push mower. When we first bought that house and moved in, I considered building a tree house in the side yard for the girls, but by this time they had become just as horse crazy as I was, and we spent most of our time at the barn at Patchwork Farms, a busy hub of Pony Club activities and Combined Training Events.

*Robber Baron, a Thoroughbred, was one of my favorite horses. Here, we were preparing for hunter trials at Patchwork Farms in the late 1970s.*

Once again, my garden had to fend for itself. At the time, I was just interested enough in gardening to order plants from well-known nurseries such as White Flower Farm. Located in Connecticut, the nursery is unable to dig and send plants until April, when we would be off on equestrian competitions around the Southeast. The plants had to wait for the horses to be returned to the stables, cleaned, and fed before they could receive proper care. Despite my intentions, those plants did not get the best start.

It wasn't until my daughters left for college that the plant bug bit. I began taking horticulture classes at our local Jefferson State Community College with some friends who had been interested in plant identification, horticulture, and landscape design. Though they were nearly finished with their studies, they urged me to join them before their popular teacher, John Floyd, taught his last class. John was just about to leave Jeff State for *Southern Living* magazine where he served as editor-in-chief for many years.

I remember asking my friends how difficult it would be to learn all those plant names, and they told me, "Oh it's just *Magnolia grandiflora* and

*Camellia japonica,* and you know them already." I knew those two, but the others were pure Latin.

In high school, I had actually enjoyed studying Latin, and that background came in handy, because familiarity with Latin is essential to dealing with botanical identification. While common names are confusing and recognized locally; it is only with the botanical Latin that everyone can be certain of which plant we are talking about.

We gathered one evening each week to carpool to that three-hour class. I hung on by my fingernails and memorized the week's assignment of botanical names by putting them on tape and listening to them while driving the car and washing the dishes. I repeatedly wrote lists of assigned names to settle them into my brain.

My equestrian interests faded as I became more involved with horticulture. My friends graduated and left me on my own at Jeff State. I proceeded to take courses that were intended for horticulture and nursery professionals, and as I immersed myself in my studies, I got to know local horticulturists and we became friends. I renewed my relationship with Beaty Hanna, who had helped my mother with her garden and who was the head of Landscape Services, the largest contractor in the state.

During the early 1980s I became more involved in The Garden Club of America (GCA) and started traveling around the country to meetings. The GCA is a volunteer-based national organization established in 1913 whose purpose is "to stimulate the knowledge and love of gardening, to share the advantages of association by means of educational meetings, conferences, correspondence and publications, and to restore, improve and protect the quality of the environment through educational programs and action in the fields of conservation and civic improvement." There are now 200 clubs across the country with nearly 18,000 members.

My local affiliation began when I was invited to join The Little Garden Club of Birmingham, which is a member of the GCA. Mother had been involved for many years, so when I first joined, it was due

TOP: *My daughters, Margaret (left) and Anne, on a riding vacation in Ireland.*

ABOVE: *Our house on Heathermoor Road.*

OPPOSITE: *Evergreen Dogwood* (Cornus capitata).

more to Mother's expression of nepotism than to my overwhelming interest in gardening. Back then I was much more interested in horses than horticulture, but I diligently held a series of offices, from conservation chairman, treasurer, program chairman to president, as I gradually learned more about the plant world.

It wasn't until later that I became more deeply engaged in horticulture. My growing knowledge made me a much better and more passionate member of my local garden club. After serving as club horticulture chairman, I was asked to be the representative to the National Horticulture Committee for Zone VIII (Alabama, Georgia, South Carolina, Florida). My new post involved quarterly meetings at GCA headquarters in New York City, plus a Zone meeting in a rotating city with a GCA club acting as host. I must have exhibited enthusiasm for this work because I was then asked to be chairman of the National Horticulture Committee, which gave me pause. After much reflection, I decided that this was an opportunity to change what many considered to be a heavy burden to one that was pleasant and fun, so I accepted the challenge.

It is always more fun to work with people who share your interests. Some of the members of the horticulture committee were experts—seasoned hands who had been involved for many years; some were young enthusiasts eager to get their hands dirty. They were and are all volunteers, dedicating their interests and resources to education, both for us and the public. Most of our flower shows are open to the public so that anyone who wishes can see the newest styles of arrangement in floral design while exploring the horticultural section's examples of plants, both potted and cut specimens, that have been grown to perfection.

Another strong movement in the GCA is conservation of our local and national natural resources. A maxim quoted by the conservation committee members is "Think Globally, Act Locally." We need to preserve and protect our native treasures before they are buried under shopping centers and parking lots. As an example, the GCA has been actively working since the 1930s to save the redwoods in California and to protect wild-dug bulbs throughout the Mediterranean.

When you have the responsibility of a national committee job and must make speeches all over the country, you have to give the impression that you know at least something of what you are talking about. I wanted to emphasize that plants have specific needs in specific places, so I became interested in local advice. This interest led me to seek out publications for specific regions—the more specific the better. I needed to broaden my appreciation of plants and planting, whether I was talking to people in Birmingham or Kansas City or Tacoma. You can't know everything, but you can encourage people to learn to distinguish what plants will do well in which area and which plants they shouldn't bother with in their own

TOP: *GCA Meneice Conference: from left: Ellen Petersen, Millbrook Garden Club, Zone III, Chairman of GCA Horticulture Committee, Mary Evelyn McKee, Red Mountain Garden Club, Chairman of Meneice Conference, Louise Wrinkle, Little Garden Club of Birmingham, Speakers Chairman.*

ABOVE CENTER: *National Horticultural Conference named for Shirley Meneice, center, held in Birmingham in 2010. Virginia Almand, left, Cherokee Garden Club, Zone VIII, and her sister, D.D. Martin, Honorary Member, were speakers for the three-day meeting.*

ABOVE: *Norman Johnson shows conference visitors around my garden.*

backyards. We all fall back on "right plant, right place."

Even in close proximity, there is an infinite variety of environments for plants. They all have their own preferences of light, shade, pH, moisture, and texture of soil. It is up to us to figure out what they want and need. There is a well-established thought among gardeners that you shouldn't give up on a plant until you have tried it in at least three different places or, in other words, killed it at least three times.

As chairman of the GCA Horticulture Committee, I was also trying to emphasize the pleasure rather than the pain of growing things. Many members are exceedingly talented artists in floral arrangements, but sometimes we growers feel that the arrangers assume that the flowers come from the coolers at the wholesale florist, just as children think that milk comes from the grocery store. I worked to develop a wider appreciation among all our members for the whole process of gardening, from propagation all the way through to the final display.

I was honored to bear responsibility for this elevated position within the GCA, but I came to earth by reminding myself that this was only one of several important committees and that this appointment only lasted two years. But what a responsibility for those two years! And in the back of my mind (or perhaps the front?) I was afraid that someone might come to Birmingham to visit, expecting a more polished garden than the one I had been neglecting at Heathermoor Road while traveling for the GCA.

I wanted to spread enthusiasm for propagation, for growing our own plants, and for knowing how to identify them. In the mid-1980s, there was an established program called the Plant Exchange, or PX, in which each of the nearly 200 clubs across the country would propagate six hardy plants for exchange at the GCA Annual Meeting, held each year in a different city. At the meetings, we displayed these plants in hotel ballrooms for members and the public to study. A card accompanied each one giving details of the plant and its propagation method. They were not judged but evaluated by local professionals who always came away with admiration for these successful efforts from a group of amateur women. It was a wonderful built-in stimulus for learning propagation techniques and a great source of good plant material to be shared between our members across the nation.

My GCA travel gave me both an opportunity and a responsibility. It was a chance to meet outstanding people dedicated to the organization and experienced in growing and showing. It became a pleasure to pass along my

*Flower Shows take GCA judges across the country. Exhibits of both cut and potted material show a tremendous variety and uniform containers allow attention to be focused on the plants. Here, carefully grown horticulture specimens are displayed to their best advantage in Houston and Palm Beach.*

*Although I am careful to leave the dramatic flower arranging to those possessing the necessary talents, I am relaxed enough at home to forget the rules and create my own displays for family and friends.*

ARRANGEMENTS IN FRONT HALL, LEFT TO RIGHT: *Subtlety is forsaken with crimson amaryllis at Christmastime. A mixture of summer flowers includes yellow ginger lilies, blue salvia, and rosy dahlias. Bare branches, pinecones, and tulips (which will change position to follow the light) comprise a minimalist spring arrangement. Early fall provides a mixture of complementary-colored dahlias. My friend Betty Brower gave me a pine stump large enough to slice into this striking and versatile base.*

education. For the really dedicated members, GCA travel is often seen as a chance to acquire new plants. As one of my friends says, "Plants are the best souvenirs of a trip." How wonderful to be reminded of people and places visited when we enjoy a particular plant at home.

Before the airlines' severe carry-on restrictions, we travelled with all sorts of plants. You could recognize well-dressed ladies in airports carefully carrying boxes or baskets of cut material to be entered in a GCA flower show. Provided you can still carry them, plants require little preparation. If potted, wrap the pot to secure the soil from falling out if it is turned sideways. Put the pot in an appropriately-sized box with newspaper wedged

in the corners to keep it steady. Enclose box and plant in a plastic or other bag with handles. If you want to store it in the overhead bin, be sure that the plane's overhead light is cool to the touch so it does not heat the space and cook the plants. The safest place is probably in your lap or at your feet. For cut branches, wrap them in newspaper and stuff them into an old suitcase so they don't move, and send them along in checked baggage. They come out surprisingly well—even better if each stem end is inserted into an orchid tube with water to ensure transpiration.

My attention to horticulture led me to join the Judging Program to become a GCA horticulture judge. Flower shows are generally comprised of two main categories: floral design and horticulture. Training to become a judge of either category is a long process, taking years of study and practice judging. Included in this program is attendance at yearly programs where candidates and prospective judges listen to more experienced judges speak. Enlisting in this program requires one to learn as much as possible about plants and how they grow.

As the British horticulturist Gertrude Jekyll said, "I have learned much, and am always learning, from other people's gardens, and the lesson I have learned most thoroughly is, never to say, 'I know–' there is so infinitely much to learn."

*All gardens are a form of autobiography.*

• Robert Dash, *Notes from Madoo* •

# 3

# YOU CAN GO HOME AGAIN

As the years went by and Mother became less active, I began to oversee much of what went on at my parents' house and garden on Beechwood Road. Gradually, our roles changed. Mother, who had been one of the most forceful, independent people I have known, became dependent on others, mainly me. I became the decision maker. Many summer days were spent moving hoses and sprinklers around at both our house and theirs, because sprinkler systems were not yet common here. I am not good at looking ahead, so I never thought much about future plans or what role I would assume.

After my parents died, Daddy in late 1985 and Mother in early 1986, it took my husband and me a long time to decide whether we wanted to return to my childhood home. My sister Kitty was comfortable in her house on East Briarcliff Road and had no interest in moving here. John and I enlisted her son, my nephew Rucker Durkee, as live-in custodian while we mapped out a plan. We quickly realized we needed an architect to help us, because newer living styles demanded structural changes.

The 1938 plans put the cook in the back of the house, and the owners in the front. At that time, cooks were given monastic rooms and only enjoyed Thursdays and every other Sunday off. If they did go home at night, the dinner hour was determined by the bus schedule. For us to take the house, we needed a new configuration for present times.

---

*I added the Belgian Fence of native crabapple* (Malus angustifolia) *to my mother's original Sunken Garden.*

We went through budget discussions, agonized over prices, and at last made the decision to buy out Kitty's half. Only then did we proceed to make 2 Beechwood Road our own. It was thrilling to be able to make meaningful decisions on what was now my property.

The first thing I did to establish ownership was to take down a giant magnolia *(Magnolia grandiflora)* that Mother had planted down by the street soon after they built the house. For years she complained about Marshall continually cutting it down with the lawn mower. Finally, he learned to leave the magnolia alone and it grew. And grew. And grew! It became so large that it dwarfed the house, monopolized the front yard, and threw everything out of proportion. Even at my suggestion, Mother refused to take it down, but she did allow it to be topped by about 30 feet. Of course, it immediately grew another top, proving that these magnolias can be trimmed and shaped with no problem. Still, it was a towering presence when we took over. When we finally cut it down, Mother's cook, Jo, cried. She had worked for Mother for over 20 years, and the tree was a hallmark to her. But without the giant magnolia taking up space and sun, other plants began to enjoy lives of their own.

During Mother's last days, a minimal amount of yard work was necessary to keep things decent, but now we were facing clearing and new organization on the outside while the house was being worked on inside. We knew that there would be rough work going on around the house, such as cleaning longstanding ivy off the brick, as well as checking roof and gutters, so we thought the best thing would be to move all the

boxwood foundation planting away to a protected holding bed where it could rest safely until time for its replanting.

The logical, convenient place was diagonally off the front corner of the house. Protected by tall trees, it provided a safe spot with high shade to heel in boxwood and anything else we wanted to save. We stripped the area clean of leaf litter, vines, and undergrowth. We also wanted to save as much mondo grass as possible and, ironically, the best patch of it was where we had decided to put the addition. This lush planting of mondo was taken up with sod cutters, and whole sections were laid out in the holding bed. Somehow, great masses of *Hosta seiboldiana* ('Elegans') ended up in there as well. They were never relocated, so late each summer, a dazzling sea of lavender blooms floats on tall stalks where the holding bed used to be.

As we were beginning our work, I was inspired by Mt. Cuba, an estate in Delaware near Longwood Gardens. It was the home of the well-known horticulturist Mrs. Lammot du Pont Copeland, who arranged that after her death it should become a public garden dedicated to the study of the plants of the Piedmont. Her decision left us with a perfect example of a seemingly untouched woodland, full of native plants displayed in their natural habitats. I couldn't possibly copy Mt. Cuba because of the difference in size of acreage and support staff, but I felt it was an exemplary treatment of a woodland property.

Influenced by Mt. Cuba, I began with a desire to use only native plants. I felt that non-natives had dominated our landscape plant palette to the expense of our home-grown riches, so I became determined to give our natural heritage the advantage. I am not such a strict localist as some who think that if the plant did not originate here it should not be considered native. I have a looser definition: if it is native to the Southeastern U.S.; if it presents an attractive picture of color, texture, or form; and if it will grow here, I will try it. If you are too restrictive and limit yourself to a certain group of plants, you lose enjoyment of so many others.

## *The Committee*

I have been extremely fortunate to work with four individuals who have been essential to our progress here. Norman Kent Johnson, Dick Pigford, Beaty Hanna, John McNabb and I have worked together, each

ABOVE LEFT: *My first expression of ownership was cutting down the magnolia tree* (Magnolia grandiflora).

LEFT: *The Committee (top left, clockwise): Norman Kent Johnson, landscape architect; Dick Pigford, architect who was responsible for house changes and many others outside; John McNabb, landscape contractor; Beaty Hanna, landscape contractor, head of Landscape Services, Inc.*

respecting the talents and experience of the others, to make a successful team. I've taken to calling us The Committee.

Landscape architect Norman Johnson had worked with me at our previous house on Heathermoor Road. There, we concentrated on small areas that seemed large at the time. But here, in this very different landscape, I didn't know how much could or should be done. Norman can size up a situation better than anyone I know. He sees everything all at once: how spaces should be organized, how to get from one area to another, how to enhance a potentially pleasant spot into a really memorable one. I had become used to the place and took it for granted; he saw it with new eyes.

*When I became aware of the similarities of Southeastern U.S. plants and those of the Orient (China, Japan, and Korea) I found it interesting to showcase these parallels. Sometimes I would plant Oriental and U.S. native species together, such as the Native Fringe tree or Grancy Graybeard* (Chionanthus virginicus) *near the Oriental Fringe Tree* (Chionanthus retusus) *(above left and right), or native Solomon's Seal* (Polygonatum biflorum) *near Japanese variegated Solomon's Seal* (P. odoratum 'Variegatum').

LEFT: *The rear view of the house shows the new room (far left) designed by architect Dick Pigford.*

BELOW LEFT: *We spend most of our family time in the new room. Dick carefully sited it for privacy and garden views. Note how tall bare branches from the Hawthorn tree give height to a bare wall.*

OPPOSITE: *A path leading to the Stone Bench curves around a bed of wild blue phlox* (Phlox divaricata).

Many people do not realize how important it is to have a landscape architect in on the planning stages from the beginning—whether building new or renovating. Often the outside gets addressed only after the inside has been planned and mainly built, even though potential problems can be solved more easily before much progress has been made with a landscape architect's help. You need a plan of some kind, whether drawn or discussed.

We did not work from a master plan. The Committee saw what needed to be done and let the land suggest the most natural way to implement these changes. The one time we had a drawn plan, it led to trouble. Norman and I were discussing the area between the Driveway and the front door. He enthusiastically threw his arms around as he described a pattern of bluestone pavers. I couldn't understand his thought process and asked him to draw it for me. I meant "sketch," but he heard "draw," and he came back with this beautiful grid of bluestone pavers that looked like a tartan plaid. I told him it was much too busy, and he replied that I was a "minimalist" and that had gone out of style "20 years ago." I assured him that whether or not I was out of style, minimalism was here to stay and it would be the rule of this place. It still is.

Architect Dick Pigford stepped in to change the old house into a new, expanded home, while maintaining the fine touch that the original

ABOVE: *Our family had lived here for about ten years before Woodhill Road was installed between us and Shades Creek. When that happened, Mother became worried about new houses being built behind us. To protect us from potential new neighbors in the adjoining woodland that we had long considered ours, Mother installed the Sunken Garden, a walled boxwood* (Buxus sempervirens) *parterre off the Parking Court. She planted hemlocks* (Tsuga canadensis) *behind it to screen us from any new neighbors.*

OPPOSITE: *'White Triumphator' and 'Queen of Night' tulips provide dramatic contrast in the Sunken Garden.*

architect, Mr. Hugh Martin, had created. Whenever we met, Dick always appeared with his handsome 6'4" frame immaculately dressed in a white shirt and bow tie. Before the days of convenient laptops or iPads, he always brought along his bulky portable computer to provide speedy drawings. With great sensitivity, he created a new, more livable home with open circulation and appreciation of inside/outside relationships. Dick was the one who realized that the most private place for a new family room was at the back of the house.

Beaty Hanna was a remarkable person whom I treasured as a friend. He headed up Landscape Services, and had studied horticulture at Auburn in the 1950s. Slim and of medium height, he always appeared in a plaid shirt and a houndstooth hat like the famed University of Alabama football coach, Bear Bryant. He spoke in a soft voice, except when reprimanding workers who'd done something wrong. Yet they adored him. He answered the phone "Yes'm," and talked while walking in front of you and speaking in that soft voice so it was difficult to understand what he said unless you leaned in closely. His car was a moving trash pile; no hamburger wrappers or soft drink cups were ever discarded. He was known for possessing a good design eye, but we never saw him draw anything. Most of us credit him with being responsible for Mountain Brook being one of the most beautiful developments in the country. He was famous for pinching plants from one client and planting them at another's.

As soon as it was time for shovels and Bobcats, Beaty sent a pair of talented, hardworking young men who could construct or fix it all. John McNabb and Rodney Decker took an interest in this place, and I was always delighted to have them work here. After their years with Landscape Services, they formed their own business. Even later, John went on to establish his own company with his son, Jonathon.

As the years passed, John became the fourth member of The Committee, and I now rely on him for everything. When we changed the planting around the Stone Circle and built the Potting Shed, he was indispensable in their planning, planting, and installation. He has an artist's eye and a master's touch with everything in the landscape, but particularly when it comes to stonework. This place is graced with many examples of dry stacked-stone walls and steps that are evidence of his hand. I am blessed that John's touch is so good and so tuned to my preferences that I don't have to direct anything.

Beaty and Norman located a man named Robert, who had access to an energetic, honest, pleasant team of men and a few women probably of Scots-Irish descent who lived down in the country south of Birmingham. Like most of the landscape workers in this area, Beaty had trained them as workers for Landscape Services. Robert's people were quick, self-motivated team players. At the beginning of each week, Norman would confer with Robert about what needed to be done in the next few days and Robert would bring appropriate numbers of workers to handle the area assigned for that day. Sometimes

many, sometimes just a few.

For our first task as a committee, Norman, Dick, Beaty, and I decided to reassess the property as a whole. Beechwood Road had become a busy street that intruded into what we wanted to be a quiet, relaxing woodland oasis. To counteract the street's intrusion, we needed to move the Driveway and block views to and from the house by raising a Berm topped with evergreen foliage. In addition, we felt the need to create an Entrance Courtyard to give a welcome feeling, a sense of arrival. This courtyard led to a fountain which produced the sound of running water to mask the increased street noise.

There had always been a spring-fed brook at the rear of the property, which was a favorite play area for us as children. Now it needed to be cleared of invasives like privet and poison ivy, and it needed some stonework for bank stabilization. We also needed a system of paths to connect the various areas of the garden. When my sister Kitty and I played as children, we knew our way around the property by tromping cross-country, but now, as mature adults, everyone needed a more civilized way to share our garden. Because of the rolling landscape, these paths would need occasional steps and low rock walls and eventually railings.

Mountain Brook has seen a lot of development since my childhood, but Mr. Jemison's original idea was to maintain privacy and a woodland feel by offering estate lots and leaving generous space for homeowners to build upon. Strict zoning laws regarding setbacks wouldn't come about until 1942 when Mountain Brook was incorporated as a city, so during my parent's tenure, we lost some of the privacy we had enjoyed because my father made a decision he came to regret.

After World War II ended and house construction began again, someone built directly next door to us. The owner asked my father for permission to run his driveway along the property line and build his garage there. This plan was contrary to Jemison's plan and later, a city-ordained 20-foot setback, but our neighbor pressured Daddy into allowing him a variance. Daddy agreed, but soon regretted it because the garage was quickly enlarged into a servant's house. Subsequent owners enlarged it again into a pool house. All the time, the expanding structure was sitting right on our property line.

As the new owners, John and I desperately wanted to maintain protection from the noise and eyes of traffic. Dick remarked that most people want to show off their house, not hide it. I explained that I wanted

---

ABOVE LEFT: *This miniature cutleaf Japanese maple was a gift from my mother. It never needs pruning.*

ABOVE RIGHT: *Any garden requires constant vigilance. Norman captured this photo of me training smilax up the side of the porch.*

OPPOSITE: *Cleome* (Cleome hasslerana 'Alba'), *the spontaneous appearance of which seemed to be Mother's approval of our work.*

this place to be a personal oasis of calm and serenity, protected from the outside, where I could nurture the treasures I am fortunate enough to have here. I want to be in a world apart when I'm here in my garden; I want to see my house, my trees, my grass, not my neighbors. You can call this snobbery, but I want to be left alone to enjoy my garden.

## *Cleome*

When we were nearly through with the interior renovations and the landscape work had simultaneously progressed, we had what amounted to a mud hole outside the front door. Sheets of plywood protected our shoes from carrying excess mud inside, and we knew this mess was only temporary. This area was not tended, and one day I noticed what seemed to be a healthy weed. No one paid attention to it, and then it bloomed. It turned out to be one of Mother's favorites: a cleome. It was white. Cleome *(Cleome hassleriana)* is a common summer annual that seeds vigorously, and the color is usually pale to deep pink. Mother had often used pink cleome to make flower arrangements in the house, in combination with the hardy pink begonia *(Begonia grandis),* but I had not seen it in years and never in white. I thought that this was a sign from Mother that she approved of what we were doing and said, "Go to it!"

***Nature holds the key to our aesthetic, intellectual, cognitive, and even spiritual satisfaction.***

• E.O. Wilson, *Biophilia* •

# 4

# THE DIALOGUE BEGINS

Some pieces of land have more to say than others. I've finally realized that many of the historic, formal gardens needed topiaries, fountains, and hedges to give them shape and definition because they were born from flat pastures. But my garden, with its rough terrain and idiosyncratic character, has dared me to respond in a more unforced, natural way, letting care and respect be my guides.

## *Driveway*

Our first big project was moving the driveway to reveal the graceful contours of this place. When my parents built the house in 1938, they ran the driveway straight out from the house to the street to save on costs. But John and I were bothered by the proximity of what had turned into a busy thoroughfare. In keeping with Olmstead's aesthetic, we decided to move the Driveway and give it more of a meandering curve down the hill. The Committee studied the proposed route for the Driveway and realized that the logical place for it to go was between two large water oaks *(Quercus nigra)* in the middle of the front yard and to feed out to Beechwood Road between two immense tulip poplars *(Liriodendron tulipifera)*. It was ill luck that this path of the new Driveway was destined to take out a healthy clutch of native huckleberries *(Vacciniium arboreum)*.

---

*After sprigging mondo grass* (Ophiopogon japonicus) *across the front of the house, it took two and a half years to fill in. Then it covers everything uniformly. Occasional cutting should be scheduled for March 10-15.*

Our nationally known horticulturist and local garden guru Louise G. Smith, better known as Weesie, objected strenuously, "You're not going to take out those huckleberries and leave those weed trees, are you?" Her lack of respect for the water oaks was clear. Our priority for the Driveway was more important than her concern for the huckleberries, so our work proceeded as planned.

I wanted to use the two giant tulip poplars at the edge of the property as anchors for the new Driveway. I found the best arborist in the state to assure me that they were in good shape. He quickly approved the one on the uphill side but he hesitated when he saw the large cavity in the other one. He said that it had heart rot, which was very serious, and proceeded to list the remedies I might consider: antibiotics, tar, tree paint, cement. None of them appealed to me. My heart grew heavier and heavier, until he said, "but it will shade your grave." I thought if the tree would outlive me, I should not hesitate to incorporate it into our plans.

Years went by with the two poplars standing as sentinels of the Driveway until the upper one, the healthy one, was hit by lightning. It was trimmed and selectively pruned, and more years went by. After a time, I realized that the top 30 feet of the tree was in shreds, ready to fall whole or in pieces—what the arborists call "widder-makers." Reluctantly, we took it down, thinking the Driveway would be lopsided with one of its anchors gone. Little did we realize that the beech tree *(Fagus grandifolia)* that had been nearby all the time would now benefit from the space, light, and underground water that the poplar had claimed for so long. This beech has

ABOVE: *Shrubby huckleberries* (Vaccinium arboretum) *to the left of a stalwart water oak have resurrected from old roots covered by the new Driveway.*

RIGHT: *Weesie Smith, Red Mountain Garden Club, eminent native plant enthusiast.*

since doubled in size to become a magnificent specimen.

As another pleasant surprise, the huckleberries we sacrificed against Weesie's wishes emerged from those same roots into another, even bigger clutch. So now we have both the new Driveway and a fine group of native Vacciniums, actually known as Farkleberries.

Beaty worried about the roots of the "weed trees" being compacted when we laid the Driveway down on top of them. He found some coarse, strong, chain fence-like material that came in gigantic rolls. This material went down first, then landscape cloth, then gravel, then pavement. All of these layers prevented soil compaction on top of the roots and allowed them to breathe. After over 35 years, the oaks seem happy.

The new Driveway served us well until the early 1990s when we were expecting a visit from the American Horticultural Society for their annual national meeting. We examined everything and found that the bottom part of the Driveway where it met the street had buckled because of

underground water. When the pavers took up a large chunk of asphalt, I discovered a huge crawfish nearly as big as my hand looking back at me. He had lived comfortably in all that water for no telling how long. I picked him up and took him to a new environment in the Brook and wished him well.

## *Berm*

In addition to moving the Driveway, we also needed a raised Berm to shelter us from the street. Beaty ordered soil in untold truckloads. For even more privacy, we wanted to top the Berm with an evergreen screen. We ordered numerous mixed hollies from Tom Dodd, Jr., a well-known nurseryman in Semmes, Alabama, near Mobile, who was famous for putting native azaleas into the nursery trade.

Because we needed so many hollies, and they are expensive, we purchased seedlings. It didn't take them long to fill in and screen the house from traffic. Among those diverse individuals that Tom sent, we noticed that one of the *Ilex integra* seedlings was a tall, thin whip. Norman placed it at the approach to the Cutting Garden, and it has become the subject of attention and comment as a straight, tall column of green. It is now well over 30 feet high and continues its narrow, vertical growth.

---

ABOVE: *The lower end of the Driveway shows a mature poplar* (Liriodendron tulipifera), *one of a pair. Sadly, it was hit by lightning and had to be removed. A nearby beech has thrived in the newfound sunlight.*

RIGHT: *Piedmont azaleas* (Rhododendron canescens) *traditionally appears in shades of rosy pink but white forms sometimes occur.*

## Azaleas

Our new driveway entrance highlighted a large, well-established grouping of native azaleas. Many discerning gardeners consider these the most beautiful of our native shrubs. I must admit a strong preference for native azaleas over the more heavily overused Oriental ones for many reasons: graceful growth, wonderful scent, and appropriateness for our woodlands. They generally grow in an open, relaxed pattern and display their clusters of delicate blooms along their elegant branches. They are called "wild honeysuckle" by some old-timers for the similarity of their scents, and most are deciduous, except *Rhododendron minus.* In the wild, it's not unusual to find a grove of the same species. They often cross with each other, so natural hybrids occur and offer added treats.

To enrich these groupings on each side of the new entrance, we relocated other native azaleas from around our property. Now in maturity, these groupings have reached 12 feet in height and they provide a show-stopping display in spring. My quandary for the past few years has been whether to limb up the surrounding trees to give the azaleas more sunlight, and therefore more bloom, or just leave things alone. As is, the overwhelming scent is heavenly.

I have never met a gardener I did not like, but I think most of us are strong-minded and opinionated. I certainly fall into this group. Even though I think all the native azaleas are special, I am particular about combining colors. I have a particular distaste, for instance, for combining pinks and yellows. The Piedmont azaleas *(R. canescens)* bloom in different shades of pink (sometimes white), and they were the dominant element in this place. There also happened to be some flame azaleas *(R. austrinum)* in the front grouping but their bloom ranges from yellow to deep orange. We already had some of them on the Brook, so I moved the flames from the front to join their brothers in the back. When we lost a big beech tree near the Wooden Bridge there, it opened up the hillside between the bridge and the Cutting Garden to unaccustomed sun, and the relocated azaleas sang their thanks. To approach the Wooden Bridge during spring blooming time is to be surrounded by their wonderful aroma. An identifying trick of yellow native azaleas is: if it has a wonderful scent, it is *R. austrinum*; if no scent, it is probably *R. candelaceum.*

## Turf Grass Or Mondo?

Once we moved the Driveway, there was a big expanse of front yard to be covered. We debated which ground cover we should use: turf grass or mondo grass *(Ophiopogon japonicus).* Grass would be a hassle because

*Flame azalea* (Rhododendron austrinum) *is appropriately named for its colors which range from brassy gold to pale peach to almost scarlet.*

ABOVE: *In England, I learned to plant the clematis in the ground and train it up to a pot or urn on top of a brick pier so it appears to be planted in the urn. Here, evergreen* Clematis armandii *in a cast-iron urn is so happy that I have to keep it trimmed back to avoid having large green lumps at the top of the brick post.*

OPPOSITE: *The abstract sculpture for the fountain is a piece of tortured copper I found in a junkyard. Smilax surrounds the fountain.*

it would have to be sown seasonally and mowed regularly. Mondo grass was appealing because it would not require mowing except once every few years, even though it would have to be painstakingly sprigged to take root. The Committee agreed on mondo despite thinking it might take five years to cover. Thankfully, it filled in in about two and a half years. Now, with its undulating sea of dark green ground cover, people jokingly refer to this place as mondo heaven. Visitors gasp at using one plant to this extent, but it serves many purposes, such as shade ground cover and soil erosion protection, plus it ties the landscape together.

Mondo looks carefree, and in general it is, but it seems to provide a good propagating environment for seeds of pine, oak, and Virginia creeper *(Parthenocissus quinquifolia)* and often demands careful hand weeding in the spring. I have learned to use a pre-emergent herbicide treatment on it in late fall or winter to prevent most of the unwanted seedlings.

I think our mondo grass has been mowed only three times for neatness during our over-35 years here. Mowing is not a simple operation because the grass is thick and tough and you need a studied plan. It is important to time the cutting in mid-March (when the new mondo blades are beginning to emerge but not high enough to be cut by the mower) and to put the mower blades on the highest setting so the old growth top is cut off and the short emerging new growth is not injured. We have tried cutting it with string trimmers but my preference is to have heavy gasoline mowers set on the highest level. The mowers should have bags attached to contain the clippings as they are cut and these bags must be emptied after each run across the lawn. It takes several men a couple of days to complete the job.

One year, the main water line between the meter on the street and the house sprung a leak. This line ran across the front of the lawn to the house and underneath the Driveway. Repair would involve digging a thick line across my well-established expanse of mondo, opening it like a giant zipper. But if we had to dig, I thought it would also be a convenient time to cut the mondo as well. We did the cut, and the dig (thanks to that wonderful invention, the Ditch-witch), only to learn that the leak was, in fact, under the house and not out in the middle of the lawn, so all the cutting and digging were unnecessary.

## Entrance Court & Fountain

Norman and Dick persuaded me that we needed to provide a welcoming open enclosure for arrival, so we created an open courtyard consisting of brick walls pierced with white broomstick fencing. As we were building this courtyard, Norman pushed for a fountain opposite the front door so that its running water could further mask traffic sounds from the street.

I was not keen on the fountain, but he persevered and I relented. I didn't want the clichéd lion's head or gargoyle spouting water into a basin. I might allow an abstracted something, but I couldn't describe what I wanted. If there was going to be water, I thought it should come from an unseen source amongst some greenery along the wall, so we installed a simple pipe to recirculate water into a small pool on the ground.

My first choice for greenery along the wall was Evergreen clematis *(Clematis armandii)*. My second and third choices were also Evergreen clematis, but, finally obeying the rule to quit when you have killed something three times, I changed to smilax *(Smilax smallii)*, or Jackson vine, which has now taken hold with a vengeance and gives a strong sweep over the little pool.

To keep the smilax in good shape, I either cut it to the ground each

*The original entrance to the Sunken Garden was centered on the parking area. We ran the Belgian Fence across and created new entrances on either side.*

May when new shoots appear or else I just cut the old leaves off and leave the main branches draped across the wall. When new smilax shoots vigorously emerge from the ground behind the wall, they look like Loch Ness monsters. They have to be trained to stay low and hug the wall when they really want to go straight up and climb a tree. They are planted behind the wall, and the new growth must be restrained with a brick or rock on top of the wall to keep them headed downward instead of up. I have to attach weights, like heavy screws or washers, to the new shoots to prevent them from climbing up. When they become accustomed to this unnatural downward growth, I remove the weights.

One hot summer day, during our first year when the water still came from the pipe masked by the greenery on the wall, my dear friend and artist Sandra Simpson called and asked if I wanted to go with her and a fellow artist to the downtown junkyard to look for found sculpture. It was August and the temperature was above 100 degrees, but I said yes to this new adventure. We dressed in hats, long sleeves, pants, and heavy shoes because this was the kind of junkyard where the stuff comes in by rail and is weighed by the ton.

The two artists were excited to find some springs and sprongs while I just sweated and listlessly wandered. Finally, I caught their excitement. I spied a mangled piece of metal that looked as if, in another life, it had been copper and had been subjected to heat and stress. I thought it should have another chance and not go straight to the smelter. I brought it home, not knowing what would become of it. When I showed it to Norman, he suggested hanging it on the end of the water pipe, and now I have my own unique abstract sculpture.

## *Sunken Garden & Native Crabapple Belgian Fence*

Mother created the Sunken Garden, a boxwood *(Buxus sempervirens)* parterre with brick walls and paths, in the 1940s. To create a privacy screen, she and her dear friend Mrs. Florence Simpson brought back three small hemlocks *(Tsuga canadensis)* from Highlands, North Carolina, and planted them behind the wall of the new garden. They have answered the challenge by growing to 40 feet, at least until the summer of 2014, when one succumbed to some mysterious malady (not the wooly adelgid, which in recent years has ravaged the hemlocks on the East Coast).

The parterre encloses beds that are changed seasonally. In the spring, tulips, sometimes underplanted with pansies, fill the voids. The tulips are ordered in July from Van Englen. They arrive in October, and spend a couple of months in the basement refrigerator to provide necessary chilling. We plant them just after Christmas. I have used a combination of late

ones, 'White Triumphator' and the nearly black 'Queen of Night.' They bloom in concert with the native crabapples nearby and are spectacular.

The tulips are a smash when in bloom, but when they are over, something must take their place. We have experimented with several different plantings, even including 'Betty Pryor' roses, but the easiest and most satisfying has been white caladiums ('White Christmas') veined in green. They give a cool look through the heat of the summer. Sometimes, across the rear, I plant a row of white, fragrant Casa Blanca lilies, which bloom in June. They need staking, but the evening aroma is to die for.

Originally, the Sunken Garden was entered by steps in the center, opposite the back wall. We closed these up and put entrances on either side instead. That left a bed about 4 feet wide between the Sunken Garden and the Parking Court. The Committee gathered to decide how to treat this space. My experts suggested a wall, then debated what kind: solid, pierced, fenced? Or a hedge, but what kind: evergreen, deciduous, mosaic? I said that I did not want to be walled off from the garden, but wanted to see into it.

I came up with the possibility of an openwork hedge of visual and textural interest that could be seen through. I had heard of the concept of a freestanding espalier, or Belgian Fence, and felt it would work here. I had my heart set on native crabapple *(Malus angustifolia)* for this fence because it's an underused native that is a four-season plant offering beauty, blooms, and twiggy texture throughout the year. But I may have made things harder on myself because these special trees are mighty hard to come by.

My inspiration was the famous pleached hornbeam *(Carpinus sp.)* hedge at Dunbarton Oaks in Georgetown, near Washington, D.C. Many garden visitors are familiar with those lines of straight trunks to eight feet where branches begin and grow up and out, forming a dense mass off the ground.

But that hedge is made of hornbeams, which like to grow vertically, whereas crabapples like to grow horizontally.

When I suggested the possibility of planting small trees in a multiple crisscrossed pattern, everyone said I was crazy and that my plan would never work. Nevertheless, I asked Beaty for native crabapple *(Malus angustifolia)*, and he said they were not commercially available. Ever resourceful, when some specific plant was impossible to obtain through regular channels, he would often resort to sending his men into the woods to dig from the wild.

To fulfill my order, Landscape Services sent over the scrawniest, puniest-looking crabapple sticks I had ever seen. Knowing that they had been freshly dug and most likely had no roots, I told Beaty I knew they wouldn't grow and didn't want them, so I sent them back. After a year went by, he again sent me crabapples, which I am sure were the same I had spurned the year before. They looked reasonably healthy, and I figured if they had lived for one season with chopped-off roots, there was a good chance that they would survive, so I accepted them the second time around.

We selected the two big ones to bookend the brick piers at each end of the space between the Parking Court and the Sunken Garden and placed the smaller ones at 45-degree angles to make a crisscross effect through which we could see the planting below. To stabilize the smaller twigs, we strung a cable between the two brick piers at five feet and wove their top branches along this wire.

When I look at the photographs taken during installation, I wonder if my advisors who had called me crazy weren't right. Those little switches looked pretty wimpy. But we have to gamble and have faith that plants will grow. We must give them a chance to prove themselves.

*In spring, crabapples* (Malus angustifolia) *appear pink in bud and open to white. Despite an unwarranted amount of time in the ground for the short spurt of spring bloom, tulips really get your attention.*

Each year the crabapples have gotten better. After almost 30 years, it is a breathtaking sight to see the dense, delicate pink blooms in the spring. In winter, I find the rough, irregular growth similarly attractive. I like to leave some twigs on the trunks to add texture to the fence's irregularly-shaped windows. When one of my garden workers thought to neaten things up and stripped all trunks bare, it took years to regain the look I wanted.

On occasion, we have had to replace several of the smaller crabapples. Much as we would want, nothing stays the same. Plants grow, develop, age, and sometimes die while under your care. One year, I noticed a weak point in the horizontal line atop the smaller crabapples and assumed it was due to a lack of sun. I thought the branches in the big tree on the right were shading those underneath. Closer inspection revealed that two of the smaller trees were completely dead, so they were replaced, again planted at 45 degrees, and they are progressing nicely.

Since I planted my little switches, commercial availability of native crabapple has improved only a little. When I have found them, I have planted them in holding beds. In March 2012, a tree demolished the Wooden Bridge and took down the wonderful sculpted crabapple leaning over it. It helps to have extras waiting in the wings.

The long, narrow bed underneath the crabapples has had a variety

of treatments. It began with a ground cover of white periwinkle *(Vinca minor* 'Alba'). In following years, that was replaced by a succession of dark and light sweet potato vine *(Ipomoea sp.)* and then pansies *(Viola sp.)*. For several years, I used tulips to replicate those planted in December in the Sunken Garden to bloom in concert with the crabapples. In recent years, rather than so many seasonal changes, I have simplified, leaving black mondo *(Ophiopogon planiscapus* 'Nigrescens') in place year-round. It is sturdy, carefree, and makes a statement.

ABOVE, LEFT: *The Brook after clearing and before our stone work began.*

ABOVE, RIGHT: *It took a lot of men, machines, and relocated boulders to make the Brook look so natural. Ironically, this beautiful boulder was later smashed when an enormous poplar fell on it during a storm.*

OPPOSITE: *During the Brook restoration, I focused on highlighting the enormous slabs of rock that created its foundation and natural waterfalls. Various ferns populate the banks along with walking iris* (Neomarica northiana) *and Jack-in-the-pulpit* (Arisaema triphyllum).

## *Brook*

The Brook has always been my favorite place at 2 Beechwood Road. In my early years here, Kitty and I found endless fascination with it. The water is constant and clear, and we would catch salamanders and crawfish and make small, temporary dams to collect water into a pool.

The source of the brook is a spring which trickles out from a hidden source between some rocks about a hundred yards upstream from our property. We almost didn't have this treasure. When my father bought the two estate lots from Mountain Brook Land Company, they were each about an acre. The land rolls gently down a long hill to the flat before the creek on one side and then steeply down to a ravine at the back. This first purchase did not include the Brook, but later he thought he should secure that little scrap of land as a buffer, even though it was considered unbuildable. (Nowadays, people in land-locked Mountain Brook are so eager for land that they manufacture acreage by installing pipes to divert surface water and filling in ravines with dirt, creating the false impression of stable, buildable land.)

When we began our work here, the Brook was not visible from the house, but I knew its potential because of the many hours Kitty and I had enjoyed playing in and around it as children. In Mother's later years of inactivity, it became filled with privet, honeysuckle, and poison ivy. I thought the only possibility of clearance would be from either the Army Corps of Engineers or the Boy Scouts, but Robert's little army of landscape workers attacked it with axes and machetes. It took two weeks to clear. There was too much debris to haul away, so I had to get a permit from the Mountain Brook Fire Chief to burn it.

Once we'd freed the Brook from the strangling invasives, I could walk it as I had when I was a child. Over the years, the water had exposed great slabs of rock in several areas, and I could see that the banks needed to be stabilized. We began adding stonework to hold them in place. Norman guided Beaty's men to bring in heavy machinery so we could define the edges of the Brook with enormous stones whose irregular beauty gave it a

much more distinctive character. I still wonder where Beaty found those stones and how he knew which ones would be exactly right. It didn't take long for suitable ferns and moisture-loving shrubs to become established in the low rock walls we built alongside the banks.

While working on the Brook, I encouraged the use of a light hand. Streams have lives of their own and will not stand to be dictated to by mere humans. I've often said to those working on the Brook that if anyone interfered with it enough to force it underground, I would kill them.

Working with a crew, it's not unusual for conflicts to arise. Robert, the foreman of the Brook crew, employed a big, strapping man named Patrick whose curly red hair hinted at his Scots-Irish heritage. Patrick seemed to handle rock work better than anyone else, so I preferred him to do that part of the job. Robert warned me that Patrick was no good, that he was a liar and a thief and needed to go. But, the satisfactory treatment of rock work along the Brook was more important to me than Patrick's record, and I insisted that he continue. Robert threatened to pull everyone off if he stayed. When I announced Patrick as the chief Brook worker, Robert fulfilled his threat and left with his crew well before we were finished.

I should have listened to Robert. It turned out that Patrick had previously been married to the daughter of one of my neighbors. In their divorce decree, Patrick was restricted in how close he could come to his ex-wife. Since her family lived nearby, he was in danger of being hauled off by the sheriff if he was discovered working in my backyard.

We also had trouble with one of Patrick's co-workers, Scott. One day, when the Mountain Brook police showed up on Woodhill Road, they told me they had picked up Scott because he was wanted on an overdue ticket for driving with an expired license in the nearby city of Leeds. To relieve his charge so he could get back to work, I took $200 to the Leeds City Jail to cover his fine. When I got there, it was clear that he was a frequent

*This diptych shows the extra path that Norman suggested adding beyond the Wooden Bridge. I'm thankful for his vision.*

visitor (He had just sent word to his father to bring him cigarettes.). In my naiveté, I got him to sign an agreement that he would work for me to pay off the $200.

When I got home from Leeds, Patrick was loading my brand-new wheelbarrow onto his truck with the explanation that it needed a new tire. I never saw Patrick, Scott, my $200, or my wheelbarrow again. Thankfully, when Robert heard that Patrick was no longer in the picture, he returned with his crew to finish the job. Neither Robert nor I ever referred to this episode again, and work went on as before—minus the troublemakers.

## *Paths & Bridges*

From the first, we wanted the paths to provide access to different areas without calling attention to themselves or their destinations. Visitors often think that there is more than two-plus acres here. I think because we can't see the horizon, we are fooled into thinking there is more space here than there really is. If, like Louis XIV at Versailles, our gaze to the horizon encompasses many acres, we tend to dismiss the scope of land, but if we can only see a few dozen yards in front of us, we're busy figuring out where we are and tend to over-emphasize the acreage at hand.

Norman laid out the course of the paths, which sometimes changed even after preparations had begun. Since we were not following a master plan and were instead working by instinct, we were not obligated to one choice. Norman is a genius at sizing up intersecting grades. The slope above the big anchor beech tree on the Brook and below the hemlocks behind the Sunken Garden was imposing, and there had to be intersecting paths on it for easy navigation. He could figure the cross cuts and curves, which were beyond my comprehension.

During the layout of the paths, I became a great admirer of the Bobcat, a landscape machine like a baby bulldozer. With its changeable blade, it can go everywhere and do nearly everything needed. With its talented operator, Junior Parks from Landscape Services, the Bobcat cleared the years of leaf litter and cut the paths across the virgin woodland, preparing

them to accept the crushed limestone gravel base, referred to as "8910."

As we progressed down the hill to the Brook, Norman indicated a path on our side up toward our northern property line, and he proposed crossing the Brook and coming back on the other side, which would require the addition of two bridges. I remember telling him that a path on the far side was "too much sugar for a dime." I couldn't let go of my Depression thrift, and after all these years, I was still holding back. But, just as he had with the fountain, he convinced me that he was right. I think now how circumscribed we would be if I had not listened to his recommendations. We would not have the advantage of enjoying the Brook from both sides, and we would not have either our Wooden or our Stone Bridge.

When we turned our attention to the bridges, another blessing came to me in the form of artist David Fuqua, who, like most of the others, had worked for Beaty Hanna. David has an artist's eye and can construct something out of native material to make it look as if it grew instinctively. David constructed the first bridge over the Brook, with 2-x8-foot pressure-treated pine planks for the floor and rough native red cedar *(Juniperus virginiana)* for rails. He left the bark and twigs intact, so they continued to give natural-looking texture while providing support. David has replaced what we call the Wooden Bridge twice, once when a tree fell on it, and another time when it decayed from age after more than ten years.

ABOVE: *After Norman persuaded me to continue the path across the Brook with the Wooden Bridge, we needed return access. He found this large, triangular stone which lies flush with the path. My Stone Bridge looks as if it has always been there.*

OPPOSITE TOP: *This iron railing was carefully designed to match the curve of the long, winding steps below the terrace.*

OPPOSITE BOTTOM LEFT: *The first attempt at a railing didn't follow the curve of the path. To correct it, we used PVC pipe to create a new template.*

OPPOSITE LEFT: *Our uneven topography required banks of steps to help us navigate the paths throughout the garden.*

Once we crossed over to the other side of the Brook, we needed a way to come back. Norman provided that return at the base of a mature beech tree *(Fagus grandifolia)* by setting another gigantic irregular stone with the help of several men and several large machines. In 1995, Hurricane Opal's winds felled huge trees across the Brook, decimating the whole area that the renegade Patrick and others had worked on. Fortunately, the storm missed the Stone Bridge.

## Steps and Railings

After many surface washouts, we realized that we needed ranks of steps when the grade changes. To remedy the problem, we used handsome sandstone slabs. Once again, John McNabb provided his expertise. He chose Oneonta Stone, a soft, buff-colored sandstone with sometimes hints of orange or ivory, culled from quarries near the town of Oneonta, north of Birmingham. Larger slabs, roughly 4-feet wide and 4-inches thick, are more uniform in size in some places. Elsewhere, he chose random sizes that he fit naturally into the hillside.

Even after John had laid flagstone steps behind the Sunken Garden under the hemlocks, I realized that everyone going up and down was more surefooted than I, so a bannister, for me at least, seemed a good idea.

Recalling David Fuqua's talent for building the Wooden Bridge, I commissioned him to build sections of natural cedar railings alongside ranks of steps scattered throughout the place to offer security to visitors and homeowners alike.

Crafting a rail is a year-long (or even longer) process. First, David measured the drop or curve of the steps. To provide a top rail to match that curve, he selected the appropriate-growing red cedar trees *(Juniperus virginiana)* and tied them into that curve with string and stakes. After

forcing the trees to grow into that shape, he cut them, brought them here, and set them in place as the top rail.

While the railings in the woods are constructed of native red cedar to keep a natural look, we felt those closer to the house should be more formal so they are made of metal. Installation of metal railings was simple in most places where straight lines could be followed. But I had been spoiled with the artisans I had worked with, like David Fuqua and John McNabb, and I made a mistake in thinking the ironmongers would be equally talented. At first, matching a metal railing to a curving path proved to be too much of a challenge and Ray Parks from Landscape Services again had to be called in to fix the problem. He came with a 30-foot length of PVC pipe, which could be gently curved to match the path to indicate where the metal railing should be placed. Supporting vertical metal stakes were placed alongside the edge of the path, and the pipe was threaded between them. Then the ironmongers took measurements from the pipe that indicated the desired curves, and they went back to the foundry to create the curved top rail. This time the effort was successful.

## *"Them Rocks": Woodhill Steps*

One benefit of building as you go along rather than by a strictly drawn plan is that you don't know what will turn up in the building process. When the old Driveway was taken up, we found several large stone pavers that had straddled the gutter and allowed the Driveway to be laid on top of them. This was a real find so we saved them. A few times, I was approached by some contractor-like men who asked if I wanted to keep "them rocks." I was afraid that, even as large as they were, they might be stolen, so I had them taken down and hidden beneath the lower limbs of the magnolias near Woodhill Road. That is where they ended up, providing

steps from the street to the landing. Norman laid them in the graceful curve that in the beginning only he could see. Some still have traces of tar on their edges to serve as badges of previous honorable service.

## *Path Surfaces*

To keep a natural look, we initially thought we could cover the gravel base of these paths with pine straw or wood chips. We soon learned that these materials would easily wash away in heavy rainstorms or disintegrate into fertile compost, which became an attractive growing medium for unwanted plants.

After we gave up on the natural material, we tried a succession of different kinds of paving. We learned of Stabilizer, which comes in a form like dry cement that is spread on a surface, wetted down, and allowed to set for a week, during which time it changes from a Jello-like substance into hard paving. It should last for years, but here it worked for only a year or two. Like the imitation stucco called Dryvit, Stabilizer (manufactured in dry Arizona) disintegrated in our heavy Alabama rains.

Next we tried a composite gravel we referred to as Red Rock, which many homeowners and local parks still use. It is a terra-cotta color and looks like crushed brick, and I am not sure of its composition. At first it seemed to be suitable: available locally, easily spread on the required surface, and compactable. But it, too, proved to be susceptible to erosion. Our terrain is constantly changing, up hill and down dale, and our rains seem to be constantly increasing in volume. In addition, I've begun to wonder whether there is something in the makeup of Red Rock that is detrimental to growing plants. In the areas where it was used or washed over, my plant growth is less than vigorous.

I finally got fed up with replacing paving material with each heavy rain and decided to do something drastic. I looked into possibilities and decided that flagstone paving would retain the natural look. I knew that John McNabb, my landscape contractor and an excellent stone mason, was the obvious choice to execute it. But when I found how expensive it would be to set flagstone over all the paths, I realized that we would have to go to another cover. (Norman once measured the total extent of the paths with a surveyor's wheel and came up with a half-mile.) I compromised: attractive, irregular flagstone at the front and around the house; asphalt in the back and around the Brook. John Wrinkle gave the ultimate compliment to the common asphalt after his inspection, "Well, it's not as bad as I thought it would be." Now, it is such a relief to hear the rain come thundering down and realize that we don't have to rush out and re-cover the paths wherever the grade changes. The asphalt is a proven winner, requiring few repairs. Occasionally, extra-vigorous plants like *Equisetum* or variegated Solomon's Seal (*Polygonatum odoratum* 'Variegatum') will poke up through the surface, or a big tree's fall will puncture it. But in general, the expense of paving is money well spent.

## *Benches*

People ask: "Which is your favorite place to sit and admire the garden?" I have to answer that I am usually too busy to stop and sit, and if I do, I see something that needs attention, so that interrupts my relaxation.

My benches follow my general dicta around the garden. I only use materials like stone or wood that would naturally occur here. It is no surprise that I have found that stone benches hold up best. I used several wooden ones alongside the midsection of the Brook, but over time they decayed and had to be replaced. I asked Beaty to help me place a new one midway between the terrace and Woodhill Road. One day, his jack-of-all-trades, Ray Parks, showed up with a big, beautiful, irregular sandstone boulder about 7 feet long and 3 feet wide, which ended up on my sight line from the house, just as I had wanted. I was amazed that two men could maneuver that weight with no machinery, but Beaty had told them to place it there and they did.

Another stone bench is in the Sunken Garden. Mother had located her statue of St. Fiacre, the patron saint of gardeners, against the center of the back wall. When we moved him to overlook the garden from a perch above the Parking Court, it left a hole. We needed a bench where he had previously stood.

I left for a short GCA trip and gave instructions to create a simple stone seat, emphasizing that I wanted the workers to use as few stones as possible and to show no mortar. I returned to see their new construction which looked like Taliesen West, Frank Lloyd Wright's western school, with its straight edges of stacked stones mortared into a rigid square shape that looked machine-made. Finally, after several attempts, under my critical eye, our last effort was successful. Now my bench is made of three large, irregular, moss-covered stones which provide a base, a seat, and a back. Simple, functional, organic. I don't want anything here except those elements that look as if they belong. As Russell Page says, "It must be inevitable."

Sometimes design can be happenstance. One of the workers called Spencer was

ABOVE TOP TO BOTTOM: *A single sandstone boulder; My crew's unsuccessful attempt at a bench in the Sunken Garden. We replaced it with the minimalist bench made of three stone slabs (base, seat, and back) which required no mortar.*

OPPOSITE: *Spencer's Bench, covered in moss and crabapple blossoms, provides a stopping place just past the Wooden Bridge.*

ABOVE: *St. Fiacre, the patron saint of gardeners, was one of Mother's accessories. We moved him from the Sunken Garden to a place overlooking the Parking Court where he can observe most of the activities here.*

LEFT: *The path to the bamboo arch and Cutting Garden is a mixture of bricks and flagstones. Irregularity and lack of polished perfection mark my appreciation of the Japanese concept of "Wabi-sabi."*

OPPOSITE: *Layers of color and texture define the Cutting Garden. The white blooms of the tall shad bush* (Amelanchier canadensis) *mark the drop-off towards the Brook.*

older, heavier, and slower than the others and spent most of his time leaning on his shovel and chatting with his pals. However, when they were building the retaining wall on the far side at the Wooden Bridge and as they neared the finishing point, Spencer moved from his shovel and came into his own. He carefully arranged several big rocks as a terminus to the wall. I don't know if it was his design, because neither Robert nor I nor Norman had specifically instructed him, but his part of the wall formed a natural place to stop and sit and enjoy the surroundings. From then on, it has been known as "Spencer's Bench."'

## *St. Fiacre*

While I prefer natural sculptures over man-made ones, I've made a few exceptions. It is fitting for Mother's statue of St. Fiacre to remain here because he's the patron saint of gardeners, and he is set pretty much out of the way. Occasionally, I will hide something like my giant ceramic frog that most people don't see. It resides under the vertical holly at the base of the Cutting Garden. You have to be looking for it as you approach the Potting Shed; otherwise, it is hidden under the dark green holly boughs. There are no sculptured rabbits or chipmunks; I have enough real ones. If visitors miss these whimsically-placed characters, that's fine by me. I don't want anything artificial to jar the scene.

For me, the natural shapes of trees and shrubs are superior to the usual statues, such as the "Four Seasons" or Roman senators found in other gardens. I look instead for patterns created by the trunks of trees with their different identifying barks, the infinite variety of shades of green foliage, and the flowers and fruit that appear and disappear through the seasons. We tend to ignore nature's own sculptures with which we are surrounded, so I notice and highlight those.

My prime example of natural sculpture is a wonderful, mature, craggy hawthorn *(Crataegus spathulata)* between the terrace and the Stone Circle that was here before we returned. The texture of its gnarled bark shows its age, probably well over 80 years. Over the years, I have pruned it back to its main branches, emphasizing its dramatic shape. It is a four-season plant, offering us a cascade of white bloom in the spring, delicately shaped green leaves in summer, bright scarlet berries in the fall, and rough, dramatic sculpture in the winter. In the beginning, when it was being trimmed, rather than letting all the cuttings go to the chipper, I held back several 12-foot branches to use in our new family room to give visual height since we left draperies off the windows and doors. I stuck the branches in a heavy crockery jar with bricks and rocks to hold them steady, and they have been there ever since. I am not one for Christmas decoration, so I do my bit by hanging a few red baubles off these branches, put a red felt cloth under the "tree" to nurse Christmas gifts, and let it be.

If I analyzed the attraction that the sculptured hawthorn, the twiggy crabapples, and even the miniature Japanese maples have for me, it would probably reveal my preference for irregular patterns and imperfections of growth. I learned from my daughter Margaret that these qualities form the central core of the centuries-old Japanese aesthetic known as "Wabi-sabi." Like "Zen", there is no clear translation to English, but this aesthetic rests on the precepts of humility, restraint, simplicity, naturalness, and impermanence, honoring both joy and melancholy. Adherents of this philosophy sought to liberate themselves from dependence on the physical perfection of the material world and recognized that an appreciation of imperfection is a step toward enlightenment. I've followed these precepts, which may be, in my garden, too subtle for many who prefer splashy color and more lively plantings.

## *Cutting Garden*

Up the hill from the Sunken Garden, there was some sun where the Boy Scout cabin had stood. Constructed of the plainest, untreated materials, the cabin had succumbed to age and been taken down. We eliminated a few more trees in order to enlarge that small sunny spot enough for a Cutting Garden to provide flowers for the house. We started with two 8-foot-square raised beds on each side of a center path that gradually stepped up the slope and ended with a rectangular bed across the back that we designated for lilies.

I carefully selected a variety of lilies according to color, height, and blooming time, and planted them with instructions from Weesie Smith, our local horticultural guru. She knew they would be enticing to moles and voles. To prevent the animals from eating the bulbs, she suggested mixing sharp gravel into the soil. While I started with a variety of lilies, soon the butterfly lilies *(Hedychium coronarium)* pushed the others out of the way and took over the whole bed. One of the advantages of late summer, these lilies grow tall (3-6') like corn, providing a strong, course texture at the back of the border along with the most enchanting fragrance. They are extremely robust, so I am continually giving the excess away.

I put my cold frame at the back of the Cutting Garden, behind the lily bed. An open box-like structure, it was constructed from sections of pressure-treated tongue-in-groove lumber. The front side was lower than the other and faced south. Tops were glass shower doors that just sat in place and temperature-regulated arms opened and closed them as needed. Eventually we got lazy, leaving the tops in the basement, so the cold frame evolved into a holding bed on one side and a compost bin on the other.

When we installed the Cutting Garden, Norman was here most of the time, directing activities. I was travelling with GCA for a couple of days and came back to a wonderful surprise: He had instructed that the path from the Parking Court to the Cutting Garden be paved with a combination of brick and large paving stones in a pleasant random pattern. I was delighted to find more irregular imperfection, more "Wabi-sabi." Just my cup of tea.

The original beds were contained by railroad ties, which give a neat appearance. We played around with different combinations of annuals and perennials but never left anything in place long enough to become established and flourish. The plants never seemed to thrive, and I suspected that they were being negatively impacted by the creosote remaining in the railroad ties. We took them up, removed the soil I suspected might be tainted, created moss rock wall enclosures, and filled these beds with mushroom compost. There must be various levels of nutritional value in this compost, because I have found that we need to add considerable amounts of fertilizer, but the texture and drainage is wonderful.

During the construction of new stone walls to

ABOVE, CLOCKWISE FROM TOP LEFT: *Blue delphinium* (Delphinium elatum) *against the stone wall of the Potting Shed; White foxglove* (Digitalis purpurea 'Alba'), *grown from seed for white; Salvia* 'Indigo Spires' *is a bee and butterfly magnet. Ancient hawthorn* (Crataegus spathulata) *trimmed to its skeleton to act as a living sculpture;*

OPPOSITE: *Spring in the Cutting Garden reveals mixed Icelandic poppies* (Papaver nudicaule), Veronica *'Georgia Blue', and white violas* (Viola).

contain the beds, I wanted to be able to plant choice little alpines in the spaces between the rocks and asked the masons to leave pockets of soil in the voids. I had the brilliant idea of creating a contained planting environment by making a sleeve of degradable material and filling it with soil and seeds and placing it between the rocks as they were set. I even thought up a name: "dirt socks for walls." I sewed burlap strips into tubes with an open end and filled them with dirt. I still think it was a good idea, but for some reason, it didn't work.

In successive seasons, the Cutting Garden has grown and expanded. First, we added the path to the left and below, then the extra bed above and to the right, which contains blue salvias *(Salvia* 'Indigo Spires'), pale apricot chrysanthemums *(Chrysanthemum* 'Sheffield Pink'), and short and pale blue-purple asters interrupted by several *Spirea thunbergii* 'Ogon' for chartreuse foliage in the summer and orange in the fall.

ABOVE: *We have had used a succession of many bedding plants, but overall the most successful spring plantings have been tulips, pansies, and parsley.*

OPPOSITE: *Red hot zinnias give the Cutting Garden a pop in the summer.*

There have been many combinations of plants in the Cutting Garden: annuals, perennials, and shrubs, changing from season to season. Few combinations have been successful enough to be repeated. Basically, there are two plantings each year, first those for spring that are installed in the late fall, and, after spring has subsided, plantings for summer and fall. Initially, I tried to leave perennials and shrubs in place over several years but recently I have been changing with the seasons.

Often we remove and pot up summer- and fall-blooming plants like phlox, chrysanthemums, and asters to make room for spring bloomers like tulips. Given good, sharp drainage, the summer perennials can winter over in the holding bed with no problem. If leaves fall and blanket them, so much the better for insulation.

Several years ago, Norman suggested that I make it a real Cutting Garden and throw out seeds. That year, I started with zinnias seeded in peat pots, and each year I have repeated them for a continual colorful harvest for several months. Using small, biodegradable pots allows the sprouted seeds to be planted with no root disturbance, and you know where they are, as opposed to just scattering the seeds whose careful distribution is demolished with the first rain.

No one wants to argue with success, so I have continued with the zinnias and in many years, dahlias. Some favorites include 'My Cindy' and 'Brookside Cheri.' These are welcome summer bloomers, in combination with the ubiquitous pink begonia *(Begonia grandis)* and white cleome *(Cleome hassleriana* 'Alba'), all of which provide cut flowers for the house.

One of my favorite pass-along plants was a soft pink dahlia: a pale salmon semi-cactus type that mixes well with roses, cleome, and phlox. With dahlias, the rule is: lift the tubers in the fall, store in barely dampened peat moss in a protected place for the winter, and replant in the spring. The only time I did as instructed, they froze in the garage. For years, I left my dahlias in the ground and they came up like clockwork in April and began blooming in July, continuing until frost. Sadly, in recent years I have lost them and even my dahlia friends cannot help me identify the one I want to re-establish.

For a recent spring display, I created a diagonally-separated blue and yellow array using seedlings of my friend Jim Landon's midnight blue/purple columbine *(Aquilegia vulgaris)* from Highlands, North Carolina, combined with the coreopsis *(Coreopsis* 'Early Sunrise') used for our Garden Club's seed challenge class in 2014. To add fullness to the base of the tall stalks, I underplanted the coreopsis with yellow pansies and dark purple pansies under the columbine. This was an interesting idea from the standpoint of plant provenance because we don't usually know such background of our plants. My seedlings grew waist high, far above their neighbors, and bloomed much later than I had planned.

Nothing is more dramatic than delphiniums at the back of the border, but they are not cut out for Southern gardens. Like many in the *Ranunculus* family, they don't like the heat. Every few years I will succumb to their lure, but finding them is a problem and growing them is another. Even with the philosophy of using them as annuals, finding good stock is problematic for us. I have tried to get someone to contract grow them for me, but that has not worked out. At first, I wanted to keep the color palette in the Cutting Garden in the white, gray, purple, and blue tones, so that added an extra challenge to be sure all were blue or white, not pink. Despite the challenges of growing this plant in this garden, I keep trying because when it works, it really packs a wallop.

As years passed and planting layouts changed, a simpler pattern for the Cutting Garden evolved. The latest addition to the main back beds was made a few years ago: two big pots each containing a young native crabapple *(Malus angustifolia)* tree. They are underplanted with maidenhair vine *(Muehlenbeckia complexa)*, which drips over the sides of the pots. It is so hearty I have labeled it a civilized kudzu *(Pueriaria montana* var. *lobata)*, the poster child of invasive plants. I have been impatient for the crabapples to bloom, but I have been told that they are too juvenile and that I must be patient.

***Anybody who wants to rule the world should try to rule a garden first.***

• *garden saying* •

# 5

# THE NATURE OF CHANGE

Be open to change, because whether you want it or not, it will come. After working for over a year to transform this place, we paused and caught our breath, thinking we could rest awhile. We never imagined the catastrophic storm that was just on the horizon.

## *Tornado*

Our first major storm was in the spring of 1989, just one year after we'd finally finished all the work outside and inside and moved in. I was serving as Director of The Garden Club of America for Zone VIII, so I was at a Zone Meeting in Greenville, South Carolina.

That evening, shortly before a dinner party, I received a frantic call from John, back in Alabama, who could barely talk he was so upset. He told me that we had had a tornado that day, which had taken down several large, old trees. He was helpless to deal with such a catastrophe. He was the lawyer who was in his element with wills and trusts, who was comfortable on the inside looking out, or if outside, with his feet on asphalt, one who appreciates a beautiful garden but is ignorant of how to keep it that way. He felt that since he was at home alone, he was responsible for dealing with the recovery and that made him very uncomfortable. He needed me there, so I frantically made plane reservations to leave at 6:00 a.m. the following morning.

The destruction was beyond comprehension. The south side of our property was a twisted, broken mass of trunks, limbs, and leaves. To the immediate view, you couldn't tell what was what because everything was topsy-turvy, and it seemed more trees were lying down than standing straight up. Chain saws were going full blast.

Even though it was mid-April, it was terribly cold. The tornado had blown all the warm air out and brought winter back in again. Beaty was already on the scene and had ordered a crane to prevent more damage when removing the fallen giants. He was supervising everything, but in typical generous fashion, he had given his jacket to one of his workers whose coat had been stolen at the hospital while he was awaiting the birth of his child. I looked in our closets and found the two down coats my girls had worn and loved during high school. Beaty wore the dark red one and I wore the tan one.

My Christmas card that year shows me in the down coat out watching the work with a giant crane in the background. The caption reads: "Why is this woman smiling?" Inside reads: "After the tornado, she will have sun in her garden." The area where the large trees fell and came out became known as Tornado Alley. This is the one place in my woodland garden that gets enough sun to create a meadow.

It is frustrating to try to photograph fallen trees, particularly when the leaves are out, because all you can see is masses of broken sticks and greenery. There are no landmarks or points of orientation to help locate you. Back then, we called it a tornado, but now those sudden, localized storms are referred to as straight-line winds. I suspect this name change was driven by the fact that the insurance companies are less liable for

*Miniature cut-leaf Japanese maple* (Acer palmatum) *in full fall color.*

ABOVE AND OPPOSITE: *"Why is this woman smiling?" Although it is always hard to lose mature trees, I'm happy because I will now gain enough sun to create a small meadow in a place we call Tornado Alley. The trees we lost were so large we had to use a crane to remove them.*

straight-line winds than tornadoes.

Another straight-line wind storm came in the spring of 1991 on Good Friday. It took out over 800 trees on the Country Club of Birmingham golf courses and turned the shady Rhododendron Garden at Birmingham Botanical Gardens into full sun. We were spared except for a tremendous beech on the Brook that leaned so dangerously we had to take it down. The next season, the native azaleas in that area responded with thanks and heavy, breathtaking bloom from the extra sun.

## *Blizzard of 1993*

On a Friday in March 1993, I was preparing to depart for judging at the Philadelphia Flower Show. There were some mild predictions of snow across the South and Eastern Seaboard, but no one paid them much attention. Snow is a rare occurrence here in Birmingham, and because the ground hardly ever freezes, it seldom sticks. It was more likely that the forecast for snow in Philadelphia would come to pass.

I spent Saturday morning inside the Philadelphia Civic Center judging the show, and by the time we were through, the storm had hit. The airport was closed; streets were impassable. In my hotel room, I was once again receiving frantic calls from home. John reported that power was out, heat was gone, the generator was dead, and snow was 15 inches deep. Everything was at a standstill. He wanted to protect the snow-laden plants but was afraid of doing the wrong thing.

The only advice provided by the television stations was to keep in touch with your airline. I can still remember the Delta Airlines telephone number: 221-1212, which I and everyone else was calling. In the end, the phone charges between Philadelphia and Birmingham amounted to more than the four-day hotel bill.

When I returned from Philadelphia, everything was white. I struggled home from the airport to find 15 inches of snow covering the frozen ground. It was the blizzard of the century. When even an inch of snow falls in Birmingham, the city shuts down. When a catastrophic storm hits, time might as well stop. We have no snow equipment and roads are impassable because of the hills. Those with four-wheel-drive vehicles empty grocery shelves within hours, schools and offices close, power is lost, and selling generators is a thriving business. Children lucky enough to have sleds have a great time, and others just grab anything with a flat bottom—from cardboard boxes to heavy serving trays—to sled down the nearest hill.

But this was a wet, thick snow heavy enough to break trees and branches. When you live in the woods and a serious snow or ice storm strikes, there is a domino effect with fallen trees. One falls on another, and that one crushes the next, and so on. Trees and limbs were down across the Driveway, blocking access in and out, but it didn't matter because

Beechwood Road was closed.

Emergency crews of tree men, neighbors with chain saws, and off-duty firemen were everywhere doing both paid and Samaritan work to clear roads and driveways. The buzz of power saws let us know that order was beginning to be restored. When you hear one chain saw, you know that a neighbor is cutting down a tree. When you hear a chorus, you know a storm has hit.

As the temperatures rose, heavy trucks could maneuver the roads to throw out salt and sand. We could finally make it up and down the Driveway. Everything in the garden remained covered with a frozen blanket. The boxwood and other shrubs were pulled apart with the weight of the heavy snow. While the temptation is to brush it off, the snow should be carefully brushed with a broom in an upward rather than downward motion to avoid breaking major branches. It is imperative to get it off as soon as possible before it freezes in place because then it is almost impossible to remove until it melts. One front-end loader scraped all the snow from the Parking Court into an 8-foot pile in one corner, and it remained frozen in place like an ill-placed iceberg for about two weeks.

The worst damage was to the Yoshino cherry trees *(Prunus yedoensis)* that Mother had planted in the corners of the Parking Court 15 years before. They reach maturity in a relatively short time and had already formed long, graceful limbs that in spring would enclose the whole area in clouds of pink. The bark, with its distinctive silver sheen and horizontal markings, was all that was left of them. I didn't know that fruit trees were weak and brittle, but these had evidently been broken by the weight of the heavy snow on their horizontal branches. These previously magnificent trees were just pitiful shadows of what they had been, and now were just irregular, beat-up, broken limbs and ragged stumps.

We were dismayed to lose them, because we loved them as a thing of beauty and as a reminder of Mother. But there was no hope of acceptable regrowth. Their presence had prevented us from expanding the Parking Court by moving the wall back when we'd first moved in and realized how much we needed the space. But now we could gain one thing by losing

TOP LEFT: *Original Parking Court with Yoshino cherry trees* (Prunus yedoensis) *anchoring each corner and creating a fairyland in spring.*

TOP RIGHT: *A heavy, wet snow brought down my neighbor's massive oak.*

BOTTOM: *Losing the cherry trees allowed me to extend the Parking Court and gain more space. I was also able to add a criss-cross pattern of Confederate Jasmine which echoes the pattern in the Belgian Fence of native crabapple.*

another, so perhaps we were, all in all, moving positively forward. I was happy that I could finally decide for myself how to design this new space and thus make it my own.

The original Parking Court was paved in asphalt. The new added area measured 48-x 32-feet: convenient space for four cars. It was outlined in a brick soldier course to match the existing one with a freestanding brick outline demarking four parking places. To me, this reads as a loud command to "PARK HERE," but strangely not everyone sees it as such. The surface was filled with river gravel, which I thought was only temporary before we were to pave it with asphalt. River gravel is uneven, hard to walk on, and can be messy, but the Committee and everyone else except me liked the gravel, so it stayed.

On the new wall, "X" marks of Confederate jasmine (*Trachelospermum jasminoides*) arise out of a bed of mondo grass to mark the four parking places in the expanded Parking Court, echoing the pattern of the Belgian Fence. This hearty evergreen vine is supported and trained on a wire held off the wall by masonry nails so the new tendrils can twirl around the wire. They must be wound around the wire or they will climb the wall. It is a hard trick to keep the jasmine trimmed to maintain the sharp pattern while still leaving enough vine to bloom in the spring with scented jasmine flowers. We also added a Kousa dogwood *(Cornus kousa)* which appreciates the sun and blooms and fruits accordingly. Just as learning about necessary sun for native azaleas, we learned by doing that Kousa dogwoods need at least half a day of good sun to demonstrate their potential.

To add to our calamities, our up-the-hill neighbor John Brock had a giant oak fall across his front yard and into ours, taking all nearby planting on our property line with it, up to our wall behind the Fountain. His house was now completely exposed to us. In order to block it out, we built up the soil in an area close to the property line and we shared the expense of planting a holly hedge *(Ilex x* 'Emily Brunner'). Through the years, the hollies have become leggy and we have added Florida anise *(Illicium floridanum)* and other evergreen plants to it so that the neighbors are now virtually invisible.

## Hurricane Opal

In 1995, we had a very dry summer and fall. In October, Hurricane Opal came and gave us plenty of water, completely saturating the ground. The winds came and took down some more big trees including some enormous oaks that fell across the Brook. One fell from our side and crushed a neighbor's fence. Another fell across the Brook, decimating the intricate rock work created near the Stone Bridge by Patrick, the worker previously alleged to be a liar and a thief.

When the insurance adjuster came to inspect the damage, he kept asking to see "covered structures." I thought he was talking about something with a roof on it. Instead, he was talking about something man-made: a house, a driveway, a wall, anything that is covered by insurance. Of course, my trees always fall in the forest, never on any covered structure. I showed him the estimate that Beaty had given me to repair the section of stonework on the Brook damaged by the fallen trees. He told me that his insurance company would laugh him out of town if he submitted this estimate, because all of this looks so natural. I asked him to look at some photographs I had made

ABOVE: *From time to time, trees fall and hit built structures, such as the Wooden Bridge and painstaking rock work. This accident marked the second time this bridge had to be rebuilt. To gain a "natural look" demands men and machines.*

during construction that would show him how many days, how many men, how much big machinery it took to make this look "so natural." As soon as he saw the pictures, he submitted the bid and the insurance company paid. By this time, it was impossible to get the big machinery back in to repair it to its previous state; we had to patch together with moderate-sized stones what had originally been tremendous ones. Thank goodness those trees missed the Stone Bridge.

## The Pond

One of my most trusted maxims is "Never assume." If you do, you will frequently get into trouble. For years, I dreamed of opening up the lower end of the Brook to create a Pond. When John McNabb and I discussed it, we assumed that the power lines marked the property line. His crew began to dig, but our neighbor quickly pointed out that we were digging on his property. We had it surveyed and learned that he was, indeed, correct. We made sure to locate the Pond well within our boundaries.

John's crew dug out a rough oval shape about 20 feet long and 12 feet across. They kept the depth at about 14 inches, constructed a dam across the lower side, and made a stone-lined wall to mark the edge of the Pond. It only took a day for the Brook to fill in the new Pond and it quickly teemed with life. It has a natural clay bottom, and there are native moisture-loving shrubs such as buttonbush *(Cephalanthus occidentalis)*, leatherwood *(Cyrilla racemiflora)*, and titi *(Cliftonia monophylla)* growing alongside. We noticed minnows enjoying a new playground. I still wonder how they got there. One explanation is that the birds bring fish eggs in on their legs and they fall into the water and hatch. I have heard that fish grow relative to the size of their container. Though there is still debate on the subject, the minnows in the Pond are usually larger than those farther up the Brook.

Some people have suggested introducing aquatic plants, but I am strictly opposed to them for fear of their aggressiveness (but perhaps without full sun they would not be such a problem?). My aversion to water lilies goes back to summer camp in North Carolina, where they proliferate in the lakes and leave a thick muck on the bottom that is easily disturbed and clouds up the water.

When we dug the Pond, the path needed another bridge crossing the Brook, so I once again called on David Fuqua, who collaborated with David, Norman, and John McNabb on the design. That engineering marvel involved a grade change, a support of concrete blocks, I-beams, and sheet steel cut on site, all overlaid with gravel and edged with low stone walls. As usual, David, Norman, and John succeeded in making this new bridge look as if it naturally belongs.

## *Irrigation and Well*

When John and I finally moved to Beechwood Road, I was determined to have an efficient sprinkler system. It took at least three years of correcting mistakes from the initial installation, but then I finally came under the protection of a friendly, talkative expert named Mike Jackson. He made all 23 stations functional and automatic, and now, most of the time, things are adequately watered. There is a clock to monitor everything, and different areas can be selectively watered or the whole system can be set for certain days or be turned off entirely.

The summers of 2000 and 2001 were killers. The drought escalated and severe restrictions on watering were imposed. I was fortunate because the first year of restrictions we were limited to the amount used the previous year, and I had used a lot. The second year brought more restrictions, and sometimes neighbors snitched on each other. Luckily, I dodged that bullet.

With two years of drought and an unknown weather future, I cast around to see about drilling a well. Graves, Inc., was the leader in the field, but they said they did not do residential work, so I looked until I found someone who would. The City of Mountain Brook had made well-drilling practically an impossibility, so this was new territory. I suppose that they had wanted to force us to depend on the Birmingham Water Works and thus guarantee that that monopoly was used and profitable.

Some think that because we are close to an established creek that we would have no problem, but creeks are surface water. What we were looking for was an underground aquifer. A Mr. Kinnard answered the call for a well digger. He was an aged naturalist who appreciated the natural order of things. He was dressed in faded overalls and a ragged straw hat, and he looked through washed-out blue eyes over a snow-white beard. He could have come straight from Central Casting. The only thing he didn't have was a forked stick to divine water location, but he seemed to know well drilling.

After close inspection of the property, he convinced me that the front corner was the place to drill, and it provided a convenient place to get his rig off the road. The rig came and stayed throughout the Christmas season before he got around to drilling in January. When it remained in prominent view from Thanksgiving past Christmas, I decorated the hood

ABOVE: *Mr. Kinnard's well drilling rig was parked behind a giant red maple on the Woodhill Road corner from Thanksgiving to January.*

OPPOSITE: *After we dug the Pond, we created a new bridge and a new path meandering toward Woodhill Road. This idiosyncratic ironwood tree* (Carpinus caroliniana) *displays its sinewy bark as it leans toward the Pond.*

with a huge red bow to show the people traveling Beechwood Road how I was getting into the Christmas spirit. Mr. Kinnard drilled for several days in January, and after reaching 380 feet, he announced that he was satisfied with our 20 gallons per minute. We were in business.

All this time, Mike Jackson, the loquacious sprinkler man, had been working with Mr. Kinnard to ensure that the new supply from the well would be adequate for the sprinkler system. The well was finished and functioning, and we were leading a pleasant, normal life. Confident that I could turn my attention elsewhere, I decided to entertain my church ladies for lunch. But nothing stays normal for long.

When the luncheon was over, one of the ladies (who must have been a friend of my parents) mistakenly drove straight out onto what had been the path of the old driveway, completely missed the curve of the new one, and got bogged down in the sea of mondo grass. I hurriedly said goodbye to the other ladies and called the wrecker. The doorbell rang, but instead of the tow truck driver, it was the building inspector for the City of Mountain Brook, who stood there and informed me that we had installed the well "all wrong." To satisfy his demands, we had to install some more elaborate and extensive wiring from the house to the well, involving several days of work and more money. But at last we were finally irrigating from our own source.

Things worked fine with the well and irrigation for about a year and a half. With self-satisfaction, I congratulated myself when I heard my friends complain about their water bills. Then the system began to run dry before it had finished half a day's irrigation. I finally got Graves, the company who had claimed they didn't do residential work, to come and check on things. From their records, they found that they had recently drilled four wells in my neighborhood into what I considered MY aquifer. So, no more free water, in a county where the sewer fee is three times the water charge.

I decided that rather than drill another uncertain well or try to get water from the Pond, I would depend on city water and hope my plants were established well enough to survive.

As my garden weathered all the changes, it began to mature into a private oasis. Rather than emphasizing floral color and the more traditional garden designs such as clipped hedges and topiary, I have chosen to cultivate the elements that have surrounded me from my beginning on this property. Working in accordance with my philosophy of listening to the land, I focus on letting plants develop as they will and tend to them in a way that highlights the subtle beauties of texture, rhythm, pattern, repetition, and sculptural elements—no matter what challenges may come.

*This seemingly simple crossing required the talents of Norman Johnson, David Fuqua, John McNabb, and a steelworker who cut a steel plate on site for the base.*

***There is no spot of ground, however arid, bare or ugly, that cannot be tamed into such a state as may give an impression of beauty and delight.***

• Gertrude Jekyll, *Home and Garden* •

# 6

# INFLUENCES

I never set out to create a well-known garden. But my efforts have attracted amateurs, professionals, and curious passersby. I gave my first official tour in 1991 when the American Horticultural Society arrived in busloads for our annual national meeting. All I could think was, "These are serious gardeners. Are they really coming here?" In spite of my trepidation, their enthusiastic responses confirmed my endeavors.

Since then, I've given too many tours to count. For some, they may visit only once. For others, my garden has become an annual pilgrimage. I've been fortunate enough to host renowned visitors who have shared their knowledge with me as well.

## *Rosemary Verey*

Natural disasters give us the opportunity to take advantage of the changes thrust upon us. Likewise, interaction with people broadens our horizons. Amidst the tumult of the storms we also received many gifts, such as a visit and friendship with the renowned British garden designer, lecturer, and writer Rosemary Verey. Known for her famous garden at Barnsley House, Verey counted among her clients HRH the Prince of Wales, Sir Elton John, Princess Michael of Kent, and the New York Botanical Garden. When any garden guru comes to walk through one's garden, it gives one pause. But when someone of Rosemary Verey's reputation comes to stay for five days as a house guest, it takes one's breath away. In the early '90s, Rosemary came to lecture at the Birmingham Botanical Gardens and had several days before her next scheduled appearance. She thought any hostess would not want a guest for that long, but I jumped at the opportunity. We had a party for her, inviting garden-minded guests, and local friends pitched in with entertainment.

Early one morning when I was going downstairs to prepare breakfast, I observed the light coming from below her guestroom door. Later, I asked her about being up so early when she was staying with someone else and had no responsibilities of her own. She replied simply, "I was brought up to make use of my time." I am sure she was working on her next book. I have many of her titles and refer to them often. Her creations of gardens both in the U.S. and in Britain (including Prince Charles's garden at Highgrove) and her shelf of well-respected titles certainly shows that she took that advice seriously. What a legacy to leave behind.

During her visit, we took her on a bird-watching expedition to look for the red-cockaded woodpecker, and she charmed everyone we met, including the staff of Dreamland Barbecue near Tuscaloosa, Alabama. She was interested in everything in the natural world and the people who inhabit it. After five days, I drove her to her next speaking assignment at the Atlanta Flower Show, and we parted as serious friends.

Clematis lanuginosa *'Candida' climbs the wall of the garage.*

Rosemary taught me many things: to keep my eyes open, to be aware of the world around me, to appreciate the gifts under my feet and above my head. She was a very industrious lady, gardener, speaker, writer, and friend. I was particularly heartened by her reaction to my garden. She was fascinated with this natural woodland and enjoyed that it had very few "gardenesque" features.

## *Betty Corning*

When I first became seriously involved with the GCA, I became a friend and admirer of Betty Corning, a past president of the GCA who was a generous mentor to me. From 1985 to 1987, when I was chairman of the Horticulture Committee, I enlisted her as an advisor to the committee and she attended each of our quarterly meetings. At the conclusion of my tenure she even went with us to England on a study tour of English gardens.

Through Betty, I became fascinated with plant families. I learned that in 1735, a Swedish botanist named Carol von Linne published his *Systema Natura,* which created order out of chaos in plant nomenclature. He developed a system of taxonomy that placed plants into kingdoms, which were in turn divided into classes, and they, in turn, into orders, families, genera (singular, genus) and species. He simplified plant names by limiting the names to two (genus and species). In his binomial system, a plant is given a genus name *(Camellia)*, a descriptive epithet *(japonica)*, and placed in a family (Theaceae, or tea family). (The leaves of one of the Camellias, *C. sinensis,* are the source of the tea we drink.) He even adopted his own binomial: Carolus Linnaeus.

Now science was secure with Linnaeus's system in which plants had been organized into families according to the similarities of their reproductive parts as shown in the numbers of pistils and stamens. Study of the flowers and resulting seed determined who was kin to whom. In the 1980s, taxonomists upset the status quo established by Linnaeus by discovering that similarities of DNA more accurately determine relationships.

I quickly jumped in and picked out my favorite plant families: *Aquifoliaceae,* or the holly family, the *Ericaceae,* or heath family, including rhododendrons, sourwood trees, and blueberries, and the *Ranunculaceae,* or Buttercup family, which includes clematis, columbine, and hellebores. It was inevitable that I'd use many examples from these favorites in my own garden.

## *Frank Cabot and Garden Conservancy*

Betty Corning also recommended me to Frank Cabot when he was forming The Garden Conservancy and looking for geographically-scattered garden preservation enthusiasts. I had known Frank as a horticulturist supreme from his two major gardens at Cold Spring, New York, and Quatre Vents in Canada, and he was a Member at Large (MAL—now called Honorary Member) of GCA at the time I had been in charge of the MALs. At his invitation, I joined the fledgling Garden Conservancy Board and served for six years. We met quarterly in New York City to discuss possible notable gardens to support and help transition to 501(c)(3) status as self-supporting public gardens.

Like me, people interested in gardens want to visit other gardens, so Garden Conservancy Open Days began in 1996, featuring individual gardens opened by their generous hosts across the country. With Frank's encouragement, I agreed to help put select Alabama gardens on the tour.

LEFT TOP TO BOTTOM: *Rosemary Verey, Betty Corning.*
OPPOSITE TOP TO BOTTOM: *Frank Cabot, Starr Ockenga.*

To convince other Birmingham gardeners to open up their properties for tour, I opened mine as well. To accommodate the visitors and their curiosities, my good friend and garden enthusiast Leigh Allison helped me train 8-10 docents per garden, educating them on the ins and outs of each gardener's trials and successes for 10 years. A yearly directory is published, giving the cities, dates, locations, and descriptions of the gardens. A small gate fee is charged and divided between the Garden Conservancy and the charity of the garden owner's choice. Leigh and I managed the Birmingham Open Days for several years, offering different gardens each year.

## *Starr Ockenga*

Betty Corning also led me to Starr Ockenga, a well-known photographer and writer who was looking for American women and their gardens to spotlight in a coffee table book. Betty suggested that Starr give me a call. After we talked, we agreed that Starr would come here for a photography session mixed in with an in-depth, three-day interview.

I was concerned about having her come at that time because the spring of 1996 was the worst spring I can remember. Instead of having one hard freeze after everything had bloomed out, we had four. We had to plan her visit in advance, so when we set dates for her to come, we had no idea what kind of shape the garden would be in. When she arrived, everything looked pretty burned, but she could focus her lens and work magic.

It is unusual for a book to be written and photographed by the same person, but Starr is gifted in both fields. She stayed for three days, busying herself indoors talking to me, taking notes from our interview, and photographing outside. It was an unusual feeling, being interviewed in-depth. How was I important enough for someone to concentrate on me and the garden I had created to base an chapter in a collection of women gardeners? It was a very humbling experience.

Publication is a lengthy process. *Earth on Her Hands* contains articles about 18 women from across the country. Starr began in the spring of 1996 with my garden. The book was published in 1998. It won major prizes, among which was the American Horticulture Book Award for that year, and it went through several printings as well. Twenty years later I still have people comment on seeing my garden in Starr's book.

We delight in being educated and entertained by garden writers. In former times, newspapers like *The New York Times,* the *Wall Street Journal*, and *The Washington Post* ran regular columns written by people like Anne Raver, Allen Lacy, and Henry Mitchell. Sadly, the schedule of these columns is now more random. These gardeners all wrote from their own experience and they mentioned where they lived and gardened. Elizabeth Lawrence and Nancy Goodwin wrote books from their gardens in North Carolina, and their readers could extrapolate to suit their own situation. We all want to grow something rare in our area just to show off, and sometimes we succeed if we give it care and attention. But we must recognize general conditions governing weather patterns across the U.S.

Some giants like Allan Armitage and Michael Dirr have lived and gardened from Canada to Georgia and thus have widespread, universal information, but they still caution what to expect in different geographic areas. For many years, Donald Wyman *(Wyman's Gardening Encyclopedia, Shrubs and Vines for American Gardens,* and *Trees for American Gardens*, Macmillan) was thought the voice of advice for all America, but he based his writing on information gained at the Arnold Arboretum near Boston. Publishers are now beginning to recognize the value of regional resources. A little search may reveal local garden clubs' regional guides that offer good information for specific areas.

## *Plunkitis*

Association with plant enthusiasts led me to discover a malady peculiar to gardeners—a term I call Plunkitis. We see a particular plant and develop a lust for it. Once acquired, we wonder where to put it and are in danger of plunking it here or plunking it there. This outcome often results in a busy, unattractive polka-dot effect. My friend Mary Carolyn Cleveland advises us to "make a statement" with groups or sweeps of plants rather than just a little of this and a little of that. Norman Johnson likes "a lot of not much." Those of us susceptible to Plunkitis might enjoy "The Gardener's Creed," which I obtained through Bonny Martin, my GCA friend from Memphis:

1. I want it.
2. I want it all.
3. I want it now.
4. If it will not grow in my zone or is prohibitively expensive, I want it most of all.
5. I am perfectly willing to forego any necessities of life such as food for my children in order to have it.
6. I recognize my horticultural dependency.
7. I recognize your horticultural dependency.
8. I will willingly aid and abet your dependency, as you will mine.
9. This makes us infinitely happy.
10. Any money saved by virtue of comparison shopping equals found money and therefore is not counted as spending.
11. If everyone else has it, I must have it, too.
12. If I have planted everything that I have already purchased, I must immediately buy more.

ABOVE: *This* Helleborus x orientalis *I propagated in the slow process from British seed. At the time, it was one of the few reds.*

OPPOSITE: Clematis florida *'Sieboldii' (top). Reputed to be hard to grow, this variety seemed happy running through a boxwood next to the garage. It even forgave being pulled up by a weeding painter and gracefully set to growing again.* Clematis *'Duchess of Edinburgh' (below).*

## *Clematis*

When it comes to Plunkitis, I am particularly susceptible to the lures of clematis, one of my favorites within the *Ranunculus* family. Many in this family prefer cold weather rather than our warm temperatures, but we are still fortunate to be able to grow more varieties than one could count. Some think clematis are difficult to grow. But if we satisfy their few requirements such as head in sun and roots in shade, rich, neutral, well-draining, organic soil, and something to climb, they are generally pretty happy.

We should look to the Brits for displaying clematis growing into trees and shrubs. At The Gardens of the Rose, Headquarters of the Rose Society in England, roses and clematis are intertwined up stone piers supporting a long trelliswork, providing a succession of bloom over many months. Also, if we remember to sweeten the soil with lime each year, they will be happy. After so many years of having to rely on advice from the Brits, we are fortunate at last to have a comprehensive reference written by an American: *The Plant Lover's Guide to Clematis* by Linda Beutler.

I have had good luck with some: *Clematis lanuginosa* 'Candida' has a large white bloom and is much more successful for me than the ubiquitous *C.* 'Henryii." I have it climbing through the multiple trunks of a Kousa dogwood *(Cornus kousa)* and in a combination of clematis and climbing aster *(Ampelaster caroliniana)* on the garage. In this latter case, the clematis blooms in the spring and the aster in the fall.

In other areas, I have put more delicate clematis such as *C. florida* 'Sieboldii' at the base of boxwoods, letting the vine romp and flop as it wishes. But I do not try this with Sweet Autumn clematis *(C. terniflora)*. That is a plant in a different category—almost invasive. At the end of August and into September, I love the drifts of fragrant tiny white blooms that cloak anything within their reach. But as soon as they bloom, I cut them to the ground. Even so, I have countless seedlings appearing everywhere, so I want to keep them to a minimum. The Sweet Autumn clematis is one that needs to be watched closely.

---

OPPOSITE: CLOCKWISE FROM UPPER RIGHT: Clematis integrifolia *(herbaceous);* Clematis *viorna type with familiar small urn-shaped bloom in shades of purple, pink and lavender; Typical pale lavender unnamed variety; Typical deep blue unnamed variety. I allow these climbers to scramble up natural railings in high shade.*

RIGHT: *Stinking hellebore* (Helleborus foetidus). *Less common and shorter lived than* H. xorientalis, *but it seeds itself easily. Sturdy stalks hold clusters of greenish flowers.*

*In gardening, the only constant is change.*

• Norman Kent Johnson •

# 7

# AN EVOLVING GARDEN

The more you know, the more you want to implement what you have learned. My growing knowledge led me to try out various installations around the garden—some out of necessity, some out of curiosity. Whether large or small, each experiment gave me the chance to use it to highlight my plants and challenge myself with their inherent properties

## Millstone Fountain

One day, just in passing, I told Beaty that I wanted an old millstone, and I asked if he could find me one. This quest appealed to him and soon he arrived unannounced, with a beautiful antique stone. We didn't know what to do with it, but we talked and projected various places in our imaginations where we thought it should reside and finally settled on a spot near the Stone Circle. It weighs some one thousand pounds, and it took several men with a heavy dolly to move it. When it got to the designated spot, Beaty would just indicate with a finger pointed, and say in that quiet voice, "Just a little over here, no, no, more over there," until it was placed to his satisfaction.

It was clear to all of us that it was not satisfactory because it didn't look as if it belonged. It sat too high off the ground. We discussed how it looked and how we wanted it to look, and the discussion took a long time, because no one knew exactly how they wanted it to look. I always want something I haven't seen before, so it is hard to describe to anyone what I desire. We had no pattern, nothing to copy. As we talked, I began to think it should be a water feature of some sort. Someone piped up, "Oh, yes, a spout coming out of the center, up about 6 or 8 feet tall!" I realized immediately that that was NOT what I wanted—just the opposite. I wanted something not immediately apparent, something you might see only at a second glance. It finally occurred to me that what I wanted was a sheet of water constantly but quietly moving slowly across the surface. We had to have a way to keep it covered in water, but I wanted as little obvious movement as possible.

It is a tricky thing to level a stone balanced on upturned concrete blocks sitting in a circular, black, hard rubber wading pool. When we finally got it set, we installed a recirculating pump in the center hole of the stone, allowing the water to fall off the side and drop back into the invisible pool below. The Millstone Fountain is a favorite installation here and elicits comments from most visitors. The birds particularly like a place they can stand in shallow water to drink or bathe. This type of water feature doesn't seem so unusual now but it was when we created it.

*The Millstone Fountain set into a flagstone path beside a Silver bell* (Halesia diptera magniflora) *whose white petals fall onto the mondo grass.*

## New Corner

Mother always said that she would never like to live on a corner. I suppose she did not want the exposure of another street or the extra traffic. But as busy as Beechwood Road has become, I don't know what we would do without Woodhill Road. It has provided us with extra access, extra parking space, a storage area for stone and gravel, and, at one time, a compost pile that looked like Fort Ticonderoga with removable fence panels.

Mother also thought that the names of Overbrook Road and Beechwood Road should be reversed, because there were no beeches on Beechwood. To remedy this situation, I planted several small beeches on the Mountain Brook Club property visible from my driveway entrance. Beeches *(Fagus grandifolia)* and oakleaf hydrangeas *(Hydrangea quercifolia)* give a pleasant edge and both can be moved easily in damp cold weather. When the city later decided to install a sidewalk on that same slope, we were thankful that our friend Nimrod Long was the landscape architect advising them because he thoughtfully designed this new sidewalk so that it meandered up the hillside without disturbing the hydrangeas or beeches.

While he was designing that sidewalk for the city, Nimrod suggested that I make a new path of my own. The original path from the end of the Driveway bordering Beechwood Road and Woodhill Road cut a straight line. He pointed out that if we moved the path, it could weave behind the large native azaleas connecting Woodhill Road with our Driveway but in a more protected and graceful way. We realized he was right, so during the winter of 2005, we moved the path.

TOP: *A hidden recirculating pump keeps a thin sheet of water barely moving over the top of the Millstone Fountain. Birds love to drink and bathe here.*

BOTTOM: *During construction of the Millstone Fountain, we excavated to allow the reception pool to lie flat in the ground.*

Taking up the path also involved taking up large drifts of hellebores and raising the whole level. For years I had noticed that the center portion of hellebores did not grow as well as those at the top or bottom. John McNabb thought it was from excess water coming off the street and onto the hellebore bed. Since this was on the city right of way, I asked if I could build a knee-high dry-stacked wall coming down from the wall at the Driveway to protect the planting from the street water. They refused, so we raised the level of the planting bed for better drainage and some protection from excess water.

There was also a grouping of exuberant variegated Japanese Solomon's Seal *(Polygonatum odoratum* 'Variegatum') that had to be dug up and replanted. They had multiplied so prolifically that even after replanting all we could use, I gave away more than 10 overflowing flats of them to friends. What a wonderful plant, so like the hellebores: one that gives nine months of pleasure, takes care of itself, minds its own business, and happily multiplies each year. Some think them invasive, but I am thankful for them.

Only a few limbs of the large native azaleas had to be removed to allow the new path to wind along behind them. To take advantage of the low-lying area, I put some black cohosh *(Actea* sp.) there

ABOVE: *Variegated Solomon's Seal* (Polygonatum odoratum *'Variegatum'*), *a 3-season plant, with clean, fresh asparagus-like shoots in spring, cool green and white stalks in summer, and golden color in the fall.*

RIGHT: *We used yellow Lady Banks's rose* (Rosa banksiae) *as ground cover on the original parking pull-off from Woodhill Road, which was later extended when the Pond was installed.*

alongside the path, hoping that its roots would stay damp enough to bloom successfully. I have moved several around through the years, and usually they survive but dry out just about the time they want to bloom in August. After many years, they have proved that they can bloom, provided they receive adequate moisture.

The path is an important link to transport visitors from Woodhill Road, where they can easily park their cars. When we first moved here, our parking area at the house was limited. Our friends became accustomed to parking on the side road and walking up either path to the house. When originally laid out alongside Beechwood Road, the path was fairly exposed to the street, but changing it seemed the natural course to take.

There was debate on whether we should be linked to Woodhill Road near the corner or could instead depend on the rank of steps further along as our main exit/entrance. I fought for the extra entrance on Woodhill, because it did not involve as many steps, and probably just because I was familiar with it being there. Each entrance/exit was marked with large slabs of stones. John McNabb and I see eye to eye about stones. We both agree that they should look as if they have always been there.

## *Stone Circle*

In 1967, my parents celebrated their 40th wedding anniversary. My sister and I gave them a party at Mountain Brook Club and invited many of their friends. Our guests knew that our parents did not want gifts, so

ABOVE: *Original Stone Circle showing the gifted azaleas. If you look closely you can see the Cryptomaria tree that I gave Mother years earlier growing between the two large pines.*

RIGHT: *New Stone Circle: In June, white bracts cover the evergreen dogwood tree* (Cornus capitata) *inside a ring of variegated hostas. Climbing hydrangea* (Hydrangea anomala petiolaris), *slow to get started, has made progress on the large pine tree in the background.*

some of them decided they would just bring plants. They were given a mass of coral and white Karume azaleas. Determined to make them into a statement, Mother decided to make a circular stone terrace in the woods off the south side of the house and ring it with these small azaleas. The new plants grew to different heights and in their different colors for the next 40 years. Sadly, by 2010, the original azaleas had outlived their lifespan and needed replacing. Since the GCA Annual Horticulture Conference named for legendary California gardener and past Chairman of the Horticulture Commitee, Shirley Meneice, was coming to Birmingham, and some 150 attendees would be visiting here, I wanted my garden to look its best.

The Committee reconvened and puzzled over how to replace the ring of azaleas. We ended up with a non-plant solution: a circle of stone pillars connected by a heavy iron chain fabricated in Birmingham.

## *Dogwood*

At the center of the circle, Mother had a glass-topped table built around an existing dogwood *(Cornus florida)*. When we originally moved in and studied the Stone Circle, Norman didn't think that the old, decrepit dogwood would last long, so we planted a very small Japanese snowbell *(Styrax japonicus)* just outside the azalea circle to provide a blooming canopy to replace the dogwood when it expired. The Styrax had come from a GCA Plant Exchange. It quickly rose to 20 feet. Still, the original dogwood remained—old and gnarled, but not thinking of dying. Several years before planting the snowbell, I had bought an evergreen dogwood *(Cornus capitata)* from Libby Rich at her Birmingham store, Plant Odyssey, and it had prospered at the bottom of the terrace steps. Despite the old dogwood lingering in the center of the glass table, we replaced it with the evergreen variety, which has never hesitated, even though it had not even been root pruned. The *Cornus capitata* blooms in June with a bract resembling that of its close relative Kousa dogwood *(Cornus kousa)*, and is not affected by rust or anthracnose. In fact, it is the best-looking dogwood we have here because it has no spots or curled leaves. During the summer of 2015, the *Cornus capitata* bloom was so spectacular I thought the tree was blooming itself to death. At the reassurance of my horticulturally-aware plumber, Richard McDonald, I realized that the evergreen dogwood was responding to the extra sun provided when a nearby giant poplar *(Liriodendron tulipifera)* had been taken down.

## *Extension of Parking Area*

When we first moved in, we created a small flagstone parking space edged with a low wall along Woodhill Road for the convenience of visitors. Then when we dug the Pond, we decided to extend the pull-off and put in a gate to access the new path. Beaty was firmly against extending the wall because he thought it would look patched. But John McNabb and I pushed and, with just the right rocks, John extended it, hiding the seam and building a handsome post as a terminus. Now no one but us can tell the wall has been added to. David Fuqua built a beautiful gate of split cedar to protect the path from Woodhill Road to the Pond. Originally, I had placed a natural turtle shell in the middle of the crosspiece but Hurricane Ivan's flood, when the creek rose to four feet over Woodhill Road, carried it away. I engaged Robert Taylor, a local metalsmith, to fashion a replacement copper turtle shell, which remains in place.

ABOVE: *Potting Shed, terraced beds and graceful steps show John McNabb's stonework talents.*

OPPOSITE: *Evergreen dogwood* (Cornus capitata) *blooms in June with a spectacular cover.*

## *Potting Shed*

In 2006, I decided that we needed a more convenient place for tools near the Cutting Garden. My favorite tool is the Billy Goat, a heavy lawnmower-like rolling machine that is a combination vacuum-mulcher. It lived in the basement, but no one took it out and around to the other side of the house to clean up leaves and debris around the Driveway and entrance area, where it was really needed. It is so heavy that it is a real chore to get up the Stone Steps. We thought that if we built a stable elsewhere for the Billy Goat, it would be reasonable to include additional space for propagating new plants. Because the original cold frame at the north end of what is now the Cutting Garden had been long abandoned and converted to a holding bed and compost bin, we decided to build a shed/stable in its place.

We reconvened the Committee but we missed Beaty's genius because he had died in 2003. I worked with Norman, Dick, and John McNabb to design a simple stone structure measuring 8- x 18-feet that would contain a big copper sink, running water (including hot water to wet the potting mix), greenhouse benches, and storage. A fan built into the wall would provide air circulation.

We thought it would be simple: all we had to do was dig into the hillside, build a structure of concrete blocks, and face them with stone to serve as the back wall to the Cutting Garden. To make it pull double duty as a greenhouse, we would cover it with a transparent roof.

As we dug, shovelfuls of topsoil were easily exposed for the first time. Trouble hit when we ran into big areas of sandstone bedrock. The City of Mountain Brook had outlawed blasting, so our men had to use jackhammers to clear the stone. As excavation became more difficult and lengthy and consequently costlier, references to the Potting Shed changed to "the Taj Mahal."

Inside, half of the 18-foot length is given to greenhouse benches, and at several places along the wall I have used magnetic strips, generally a trick of chefs to hold their knives, for my hand tools. Initially, the floor was left natural clay covered with gravel, but the gravel proved too difficult a surface to move the heavy Billy Goat around on. To make things easier, John paved the floor with a natural-colored landscape brick. It is the perfect floor: you can spill water on it and sweep spilled potting mix under the bench. Rodney Decker, John McNabb's former partner, waterproofed the inside walls with an adobe-colored mix that looks like what this is: dug into the hillside. The serendipitous discovery was that the structure, being half underground, provides enough insulation so that we need no supplemental heat during the winter.

Propagating supplies like potting mix, vermiculite, perlite, sand, and manure are kept in 5-gallon plastic buckets stored under the benches, and out-of-season stakes are kept neatly in clay chimney flues lined up against the wall.

The hillside behind the Potting Shed rises sharply to the neighbor's property line. John McNabb faced this slope with stone to match the shed. I thought that I would plant a dry garden there of succulents and cacti, but there was not sufficient sun. I discovered an unexpected pleasure. The lowest terrace is just waist high, providing an easy sticking bed that can be put to use without squatting down. To access the different levels, John brought in more stone pavers and laid them in a most graceful curve. I called Norman and told him to come quickly because I expected Fred Astaire and Ginger Rogers to come dancing down the steps at any moment.

I'm glad I'm not a commercial grower whose livelihood depends on what I grow in my greenhouse, because my orientation faces north instead of south and therefore we don't get maximum light. But it is enough to give me pleasure in propagating seeds and cuttings and nursing plants along. It still gives me a thrill to see a seed sprout; I feel a renewal of the natural cycle, and I rejoice at the power residing in that insignificant-looking seed. Nature's generous seed production allows us to be extravagant while remembering the old English adage: "One to sow, one to grow, one for the mouse and one for the crow."

When I was active with the GCA, I promoted propagation with a traveling dog-and-pony show to demonstrate how to strike hardwood cuttings by using a Styrofoam cooler as a portable greenhouse. Thanks to Phyllis Lee of Honolulu, who has held many offices in GCA, I am extremely honored that there is a propagation award in a Major GCA Flower Show which bears my name.

RIGHT, TOP TO BOTTOM: *Architect Dick Pigford helps an electrician hang a light fixture on the outside entrance to the Potting Shed. We discovered sandstone in the hillside as we excavated for the potting shed. Interior with propagating materials.*

OPPOSITE: *The side wall of the Potting Shed forms the back wall of the Cutting Garden. A holding bed for waiting plants lies behind the shed.*

***Successful gardening is doing what has to be done, when it should be done the way it ought to be done whether you feel like doing it or not.***

• Jerry Baker •

# 8

# TIME AND THE GARDEN

Gardening is both challenging and rewarding because it deals not only in the three dimensions: length, width, and depth, but also in the fourth dimension, time, which dictates that everything is constantly changing. It amazes me to think of the plants in Japanese gardens that have been grown yet maintained in the same proportions over the centuries.

We must respond to the fourth dimension of time by paying attention and doing things when they should be done, no matter where we live. We may have our wants, but we shouldn't expect the luxury of instant gratification. We must look forward. If we are planning a new layout, we need to aim about six months ahead. I should be accustomed to such thinking from my past life with horses. When trailering, the driver must think and act at least a quarter mile ahead of stops or turns, because the horses' long legs put their center of gravity high off the ground, and they can easily be caught off balance.

For gardeners, preparation is key. Plants are organic; they are living, growing, ever-changing. We have to consider the soil type and how it absorbs, holds, or sheds water; how and where the sun comes up and moves through the day; how hot or cold the weather gets; whether wind is a factor; humidity or lack of it—all of these things influence our success or failure. Once we determine these things, we must learn to what degree they are important: is it full sun, half-day sun, high shade, dappled shade, full shade? We can get help answering these questions at no cost from our local Botanical Garden or County Extension Agent. The most important thing is to stay alert to what is going on around us. Especially careful gardeners keep records of temperature highs and lows, dates of bloom time from year to year, record rainfalls and droughts. I cannot claim to be that careful a gardener.

When trying to establish (or re-establish) a garden, if a homeowner wants success instead of frustration, three factors must be considered. The gardener must know his growing hardiness zone, soil pH and texture, and how the land drains. The proper zone can be found on most horticultural maps indicating cold tolerance, and now the American Horticultural Society has established maps of heat tolerance as well. The soil pH can be ascertained by a soil test, and drainage can be determined by sharp observation during rainstorms. But the most important thing is experience. Just try it out.

If you move or sell a house, take as many of your choice plants as possible. You may have to dig and move them before the house is put on the market. We had an extra lot with our Heathermoor Road house, which had been the recipient of many wildflowers and native plants dug or bought over the years. I should have taken them or at least asked permission to dig before the lot turned into a new house and driveway.

*This beech* (Fagus grandifolia) *developed into a magnificent specimen when the neighboring poplar* (Liriodendron tulipifera) *was taken down.*

Consequently, I left behind significant plants which meant something to me but not to the new owners.

When moving into an older home, leaving everything alone for the first year has its advantages. Waiting to plant can be difficult because the initial urge is to go out and plant this here and that there, but there is usually no indication what lies in the ground over here or over there. If you can wait for the next season's plants to appear, you're likely to find a world of surprises. If you're impatient and prefer instant planting, you may be erasing your future pleasure by interfering with what is waiting to appear.

## Trees

One of the most critical judgments in landscaping is in placing trees, or anything that will grow and fill in the space allotted to them. I once heard a lecture by J. C. Raulston on the subject of "Time and the Landscape," and I thought he would begin with the present or 20 years ago and show how things change. Instead, he began with the example of Newport, Rhode Island. Most of us are familiar with the great stone piles they called "cottages." In the late 19th century, property owners wanted to display their substance and importance by the dazzling size of their homes. In photographs taken at the time of construction, I was surprised at the small caliper of trees planted. I learned that the owners thought the house would look larger and more important if the trees were small, so they used young stock. These proud owners unknowingly benefitted from their grand notions; small trees

LEFT: *Original magnificent beech* (Fagus grandifolia) *was planted soon after we moved in. It suffered from the Blizzard of 1993 and from the neighbor's tree falling into it so had to be replaced.*

OPPOSITE: *Replacement beech* (Fagus grandifolia) *with graceful lower branches. It is trying to make up for lost time.*

usually take hold and grow better and faster than large ones. In time, the trees developed into the gigantic ones we see now.

During a visit to Newport, I was surprised at the absence of American beeches *(Fagus grandifolius).* I can think of no more elegant tree than the American beech, but the Newporters evidently had been educated that imported fern-leafed and copper beeches are better.

Norman and I agree on many plants: the grandeur of the American beech is one. Before 1990 we planted a native beech in the front yard. I didn't realize how well Norman had placed it until it began to develop in the years following. By 1993, it had grown long enough to become an important statement until the March blizzard took out its right-hand upper quarter, but in subsequent years it filled in to be more or less symmetrical. It developed into a showstopper, even though it was not perfectly formed. The branches swept the ground, and in fall it was a golden fireball that exploded into our view when we entered or left the Driveway. Even the non-horticulturist John Wrinkle claimed it as a favorite and has reminisced about it to this day.

But nature wouldn't leave this magnificent specimen alone and my neighbor's huge pine tree fell and demolished it. I looked for a replacement for months, but it is terribly difficult to find beeches with limbs extending to the ground. Nurserymen don't want to be bothered with bringing them along because they take up too much space and involve too much care when moving them around. Finally, I found one in a friend's yard and persuaded him to sell it to me. It is developing nicely. Some people shop for clothes or shoes or furniture; I shop for plants.

Different species of the same plant behave so differently and you don't know their characteristics until years after planting. Constant vigilance is required of any gardener. We may plant something, thinking it's set in stone, but plants are continually developing for better or worse. For example, if you want a solid, dense evergreen hedge as we did for our Berm, you should use the Chinese tribe of hollies (those with *Ilex cornuta* in their genes) because they seem to keep their limbs to the ground much better than many of the natives, particularly cultivars of *Ilex attenuata,* such as 'Foster #2,' 'Savannah,' and 'East Palatka.' When grown in the nursery, these latter two are nurtured and fertilized, grown in open sun, and trimmed to dense, symmetrical shapes. When they are brought into a landscape setting, particularly into shade, they lose their compactness and open up more casually and usually more gracefully. They lose their lower limbs and go through a leggy stage before they finally become trees.

I learned this valuable lesson when the *Ilex attenuates* we had gotten from Tom Dodd to use as a shield on our Berm eventually dropped their lower branches, exposing us to the busy street. I planted three Emily Brunner hollies *(Ilex* 'Emily Brunner') to fill those holes and screen us once

again. I knew how this variety performed because I'd planted six down near the corner earlier. I named them the six dwarfs, because they were so similar yet so distinctive. Within a few years of exposure to high shade, they opened up and became more individualistic. When one died and had to be removed, I recognized the girdling scars made by the sapsuckers, which peck holes around the trunk. They eat insects drawn to the sap as well as receive nourishment from the sap itself. (One of the mysteries I ponder is whether birds—sapsuckers in particular—have an olfactory sense. If they do, I could protect my trees by slathering Mentholatum or some other strong-smelling ointment on the bark.)

When placing trees and shrubs, it is hard to estimate the ultimate growth. There are so many variables: light, soil, fertility. Something may flourish and grow well in some places and just endure a lackluster existence in another. Things need constant attention and can get ahead of you if you don't watch out.

## Planting

Most landscapers know more than their clients, but it behooves the clients who want to be involved to keep a close eye on their contractors, particularly when they are planting trees and shrubs. The ground should be

TOP: *Emily Brunner holly* (Ilex *'Emily Brunner') with seasonal berries.*

BOTTOM: *If scars like these left by sapsuckers girdle the tree (encircle the trunk), it will die.*

OPPOSITE: *After 30 years of trimming this* Daphniphyllum macrocarpum *back to try to match its mate on the other side of the Driveway, I finally gave up on pairs. But this one tree remained to puzzle visitors seeking to identify it. An evergreen, it looks like a combination of* rhododendron, magnolia grandiflora *and sweet bay magnolia.*

prepared and, if necessary, additions made for drainage, absorbability, and organic matter. The site should be assured of adequate sun and moisture. Most trees and shrubs are bought from the nursery either in containers or balled and burlapped ("b & b"). If they are in containers, the buyer should check to see if they are root-bound when they are removed from their containers. If so, outside roots should be cut vertically or the whole ball teased apart.

One of the main concerns is to make sure that the trees or shrubs are not planted too deep. (This is especially true for shallow-rooted plants like boxwood, dogwood, and azaleas, which prefer to be high in the ground.) All plants should be planted at the same level they have been in the pot. Where they meet the ground, most trunks demonstrate a root flare that should be visible above ground after planting. This transition area between bark and roots should be left dry and free of soil, mulch, and vines.

Everyone knows the old saying, "It's better to put a $5 tree in a $50 hole, than a $50 tree in a $5 hole." Sure, it's important to observe proper hole size and soil mixture, but sometimes we neglect other aspects. The burlap wrapping the ball is sometimes made of synthetic material that will not rot as hemp does, so the plants are set in the ground in a permanent wrap that the roots cannot penetrate. Always make sure your burlap is degradable.

Another wrap often seen is wire baskets, making transport much easier. The metal parts of the basket can be grasped and pulled with no harm to the plant. Many nurserymen will take off any fabric wrap and settle the plant in the ground with its basket intact. I recently examined a dogwood that had been declining and realized that the metal pieces of the basket had become an easy access for underground varmints. I don't know if there is any way to remedy the situation without digging and resetting the tree after the basket has been removed.

There is the ongoing dialogue about holes and how much soil should be disturbed around the root ball. Some say to dig a hole to accommodate the plant and not disturb the neighboring soil, that the plant must learn to fend for itself as soon as new roots begin to grow outward. Perhaps that is sound advice in areas where the soil is loamy and of fairly good texture. In many areas similar to ours here, we would just be digging a hole in the clay and thus producing a clay container with no drainage hole for the plant. We have learned that when possible, the roots extend far beyond the limit of the dripline, which we used to consider the limit. If the roots are allowed to extend naturally, they are able to absorb more nutrients and hold the tree in place during stress and storms.

Any serious gardener is going to try to grow plants that do not want to grow in their zone. For several years I was the proud owner of a Carolina hemlock *(Tsuga caroliniana)*. Its needles grow around the stem in contrast to the *T. canadensis*, whose needles grow flat off either side of the stem. It is rarely seen outside of the western North Carolina mountains because it cannot stand the heat elsewhere in the South, but I had one growing in a cool spot at the bottom of the steps below the tall Canadian ones *(Tsuga canadensis)*. One summer, it flagged and died, and when we removed it, it was clear that it had been planted too deep; no flare was seen above the ground.

We may study and plan before planting a tree or shrub to make sure it occupies the correct site, but sometimes we plant trees in the wrong place or else they simply outgrow their spot. Before we even moved in at 2 Beechwood Road, Tom Dodd sent me an unknown Korean specimen, some sort of evergreen with long droopy leaves. I planted what turned out to be a rare *Daphniphyllum* right beside the Driveway in our entrance court where it flourished for thirty years before outgrowing its location. Since I couldn't justify taking up the Driveway to save the tree, it had to be cut down.

Sometimes, these mistakes can be remedied by moving the tree if you have the tools and a strong back. Before any change is made to an established plant, it's important to consider root-pruning. To do this, draw an imaginary circle on the ground around the tree or shrub, not necessarily as far out as the dripline, but not too close to the trunk. Take a spade and cut into the soil 6 to 8 inches (Do not lift any dirt, just jam the spade straight down into the soil along your

line), outlining a circle around the plant to be moved. The farther away from the trunk the better, but the larger the root ball, the harder it is to move. You must decide what is best for the plant and what is best for your back. Leave everything alone for 6 to 12 months. This allows the plant to develop new feeder roots within the circle you have cut, and it has a much better chance of survival than if it were moved immediately. If your soil has good texture and is likely to fall apart, it is a good idea to wrap the roots in a burlap leaf cloth and tie it with twine.

## Shade

Someone once told me "Shade grows." How true! Before you know it, trees have grown and sun has turned to shade—especially in a woodland garden like mine. I need to call my arborist on a regular basis to thin or limb up trees to give some light to whatever is below. He is on immediate call whenever we have a storm, and somehow his men clean up the debris and re-establish order out of chaos. Books have been written on different kinds of shade and what will grow in each, but it is hard to find illustrations of true shade gardens. A glance through the internet on "shade gardening" will show beautiful covers that seem to illustrate gardens of half sun. Very few of these authorities treat areas of all-day majority shade like I have here. Of course, the different seasons provide their own kinds of shade. I particularly enjoy the ephemeral wildflowers, like trilliums, that flourish before the leaves of the deciduous trees turn the woods into shade.

The wide world of ferns and hostas are the traditional plants that help us green up many dark areas. But real, dense shade can discourage almost anything from growing. Cast-iron plant *(Aspidistra elatior)* is one that will grow in deep shade, but even it will not thrive in black shade. Lily of China or Rohdea *(Rohdea japonica)* is another for full shade. It shows its dislike of sun by turning yellow.

My favorite ferns have been the maidenhairs *Adiantum capillus veneris* and *A. pedatum* with their graceful rachis or stems waving in the slightest breeze. Some think them difficult, but they must be placed in a site that they like. I have a bank of them across the front of the house where they receive the morning sun and lime leaching out from the house foundations.

ABOVE: *Southern maidenhair fern* (Adiantum capillis-veneris) *enjoys partial sun and excellent drainage on a back slope. When you find a place hospitable to a plant, let it go. I steal from here for sprigging it in other places.*

ABOVE (CLOCKWISE FROM TOP LEFT): *Fairy bells* (Disporum flavens) *is a welcome woodland shade-loving perennial ground cover. Great white trillium* (Trillium flexipes) *blooms better in the South than the more familiar* Trillium grandiflorum. *Northern maidenhair fern* (Adiantum pedatum) *waves its palm-like fronds on tall stalks and likes neutral pH, well draining soil, and half sun/shade. Yellow Lady slipper orchid* (Cyprepedium calceolus) *is a fragile treasure dependent on mycorrhizal present in soil fungus. Sometimes they are available in catalogues for high prices which do not guarantee their success. I found these in the* Alabama Farmer's Journal *and asked the seller to pack them with extra soil to ensure obtaining the necessary fungus.*

Down on the Brook, with more moisture and less sun, cinnamon fern *(Osmunda cinnamomea)* and regal fern *(Osmunda regalis)* both grow to 3-4 feet with the same spread. They like neutral to acid soil and will spread slowly in high shade. There are techniques for lightening up the shade, such as limbing up trees. Even limbed, the trees continue to grow taller, so their canopy is higher. Lower limbs can be trimmed to provide more light underneath, or "holes" can be opened up by selective pruning which interrupts the shade with spots of light. This way you have it all: the tall canopy, the mid-size trees, the shrubs, and then the ground covers.

## Sun

The longer I am responsible for this garden, the more I realize how important is the access to sun. Most plants just don't grow without it. The pattern of flowering and subsequent fruiting on areas of plants often indicates where the sun has hit them. A few years ago, I was pleasantly surprised to discover a yellow-flowered deciduous magnolia *(Magnolia* 'Elizabeth') by literally running into a beautiful flower on a tree where I had not expected it. The little tree had grown up to the point that its head had reached some sun, and it performed as it had been programmed to do.

I also see this pattern on a 20-foot yellow-berried yaupon *(Ilex vomitoria)* we planted on the upper property line. Where the sun hits it, it is covered with fruit; where it is in shade, there are no berries.

When catalogs or reference books denote future height and width of

---

ABOVE LEFT: *Looking down on the Wooden Bridge with Silver bell* (Halesia diptera magniflora) *in foreground.*

ABOVE RIGHT: *Yellow berried yaupon* (Ilex vomitoria). *This yellow berried form responds to sunlight with a healthy berry set.*

OPPOSITE: *A large shrub or small tree, the rare Buttercup winter hazel* (Corylopsis pauciflora) *blooms with small drooping clusters of slightly fragrant yellow flowers in late winter or early spring.*

trees and shrubs, we should remember that, like the minnows in the Pond, they will grow relative to where they are planted. Many things influence their growth: USDA growing zones, shade, sun, wind, soil composition, temperature, moisture, and dryness. If, for example, they are located in good soil in morning sun with adequate moisture, they will grow to their prescribed size. If, however, they are planted in an area that restricts their root growth, they may remain smaller. There is terrific variability in plants except those produced from clonal reproduction, which produce mirror reproductions of each other. Seedlings, on the other hand, will often give you a surprise or alteration. A helpful reference for future size and shape and other characteristics is *Landscape Plants for Eastern North America, Exclusive of Florida and the Immediate Gulf Coast* by Harrison L. Flint.

Things grow, some fast and some slow. When dealing with plants, even though botanical Latin may be confusing to many of us, there are many aids for understanding these names if we know how to look. We often see the term "Nana" attached to a shrub. Technically it means "less than." In practice, it just means smaller than the more usual one. We can recognize many plants by their descriptive species name: *Camellia japonica* is a camellia from Japan, *Magnolia grandiflora* is a magnolia with a large flower. One of our prime growers was a *Cunninghamia* labeled 'Nana,' which we planted at the base of a dogwood tree and expected to stay small. It has far outdistanced the mature dogwood and doesn't seem to be slowing down. Sometimes they are mislabeled in the nursery.

One of the hardest things is finding a plant that will maintain a desired size. Most gradually increase until their inherent dimensions are reached. It is hard to find a tree or shrub that will not in time outgrow its allotted space. Some adventurous gardeners are tempted to use *Viburnum davidii* for a coarse-textured evergreen that will remain a medium size, but I have never seen one successfully grown here in Birmingham. Those with a bold spirit will try Daphne, and I had wonderful luck for over 25 years here

ABOVE: *This well-formed Korean Stewartia* (Stewartia koreana) *has occupied a prominent place in my front yard and did not begin to bloom until it was more than 25 years old. Recently a giant limb fell and shaved off the near side of it. I have cleaned it up and will see how it responds.*

with some *Daphne odora* 'Aureomarginata' planted in gravel on the front terrace, where it received only natural rainfall. Most agree that this notoriously finicky plant insists on perfect drainage and protection from excess sun and wind. Mine seemed happy. When it finally grew up and over the living room's window ledge, I foolishly made the mistake of pruning it. After that it sulked for a year or two and then died. Now I have had the same initial good luck (for 15 years) with another of the same type Daphne by the back door. It is crowding the door and makes it awkward to enter and leave. I asked visiting horticulturist Larry Mellichamp what to do, and he said, "Move the door."

---

ABOVE: *Healthy specimen of winter daphne* (Daphne odora '*Aureomarginata*') *which nearly blocks the door, but I am afraid to prune it. Planted in gravel under an overhang, it receives a minimum of water.*

LEFT: *Bloom of* Stewartia koreana.

***The wonder of the world***
***The beauty and the power,***
***The shapes of things, their colours, lights and shades:***
***These I saw. Look ye also***
***While life lasts.***

• Found on an old English tombstone •

# 9

# SEASONS

It is the quiet nuances of the seasons that move me. Texture in the garden surrounds us so subtly that often we are barely aware of its presence. It can be found in all the elements that make up our garden: buildings and hardscapes, natural elements like rocks and streams, but mainly in plants, their leaves top and bottom, shapes, and barks of trees and shrubs.

The surface of the leaves can be smooth or coarse, large or small. Leaf margins (edges) can be entire or serrated, or any variation in between. The arrangement of the leaves can be close or widely spaced. The color of green appears in infinite variety from the light chartreuse of the *Spirea thunbergii* 'Ogun' to the almost black *Aucuba japonica.*

When we notice texture, it is usually due to the contrast of one element against another, shape or color. Think of the sharply dissected leaves of the Japanese maple *(Acer japonica)* against the pointed blades of mondo grass *(Ophiopogon japonicus)* that melt into a harmonious unit. Or the delicate fern frond against the rough alligator skin of the massive pine tree. If everything is the same texture, it is monotonous. If there is sufficient contrast, it snaps.

Closely allied with texture is shape: the outline of a tree, shrub, or perennial. Contrasting shapes complement each other and create interest. The straight trunk of the towering poplar is wrapped in the gentle curve of the flagstone steps which are in turn echoed by the curve of the metal railing that follows alongside.

Most often they fit with one another in a pleasing combination, but some care is needed when making our selections. Remember that usually whatever is planted will be growing and changing shape as time goes by, and we must pay attention to keep everything in proportion.

When considering seasons, we often think of distinct times of the year, separate from each other. It is easy to divide the year into quarters: spring, summer, fall, and winter. The trouble with this thinking is that here in the South our seasons are not so easily divided; they seem to just melt into each other, and our winter is thankfully shorter than that in other areas. But still we think in general seasonal terms. I am impatient with those who talk about the "peak of bloom" or the "best season in your garden." There is something of interest most of the time, whether it is bud development, bloom in its prime, fruit in the fall, or interesting barks in winter.

## *Spring*

In the South, spring begins in January and February with the flowering apricot *(Prunus mume),* Spring snowflake *(Leucojum vernum),* and Paperbush *(Edgeworthia chrysantha),* as well as the many early bulbs.

*Curving stone steps lined with mondo grass* (Ophiopogon japonicus), *narcissus, Solomon's Seal* (Polygonatum odorata), *and leucothoe.*

CLOCKWISE FROM TOP LEFT: *Japanese andromeda* (Pieris japonica) *blooms in early spring with clusters of white to pale pink ericaceous urn-shaped flowers. Many varieties of this choice evergreen are available. Rue anemone* (Anemone thalictroides) *welcomes spring with its delicate leaves resembling* thalictrum *and exquisite diminunitive white flowers. Alabama croton* (Croton alabamensis) *is rarely seen or available but it will grow anywhere. Paperbush* (Edgeworthia chrysantha), *like its close relative, sweet smelling Daphne, perfumes the surrounding air in late winter.*

OPPOSITE: *Unfurling cinnamon fern* (Osmondastrum cinnamomeum) *croziers announce spring.*

Sometimes people look up and realize that the trees have suddenly sprouted a canopy of green, composed of individual leaves. It is almost like those myopics who put on glasses for the first time and suddenly realize that this maze of green above has infinite detail. If they had paid closer attention, they would have seen the gradual change coming over the naked tree skeletons through the winter as the buds began ever so slightly to swell and to take on color. These trees have prepared for the season to come, just like the native azaleas that set buds the previous July. I am always reassured, remembering that the plants are not sitting idly by through the winter, but that they are readying themselves for the spring and that root growth continues as long as the soil temperature is at least 40 degrees.

Among the beauties of early spring are the many Japanese magnolias *(Magnolia soulangiana* and *M. stellata)* with their white to pink to purplish red flowers that create a display before the leaves appear. The only problem is that their bloom usually heralds a killing freeze, destroying their bloom as well as anything else blooming out at the same time.

While everything around us is exploding in what Edith Henderson calls "the uproar of spring," I concentrate on my Cutting Garden, which has had a schedule of sorts beginning each year with the use of tulips, sometimes under planted with pansies or violas planted in winter, as the focal point. Here in Alabama, we treat tulips as annuals. They need a period of chilling, so when they arrive in October, they must be refrigerated until they are planted just after Christmas to bloom with the crabapples in late March or early April. Then they are dug up and discarded.

In the early years of the Cutting Garden, we had tulips planted out, clematis climbing on the narrow, pyramid-shaped tuteurs, and corners of black mondo grass. We have had a variety of plants and patterns and colors, but we seem to stay in a palette of blue, yellow, and white. These colors are displayed in a favorite combination of tulips, pansies, and snapdragons from the nursery combined with white foxglove and deep blue columbine from seed. I resort to seed to guarantee the preferred white foxgloves; the columbine are pass-along plants from my friend Jim Landon. After years of trying shrubs among the spring bloomers in the Cutting Garden, I have ended up with four evenly spaced balls of *Spirea thunbergii* 'Ogon' in the upper bed, interspersed with

phlox, asters, and chrysanthemums for fall. This is the first spiraea to bloom in the spring and turns a wonderful orange gold in the fall.

Narcissus offers us a tremendous variety of bloom time, from early, midseason to late, as well as size, from the large trumpet King Alfreds to the species miniatures like the delicate, fragrant *N. jonquilla simplex.* They are a bargain because, being distasteful to deer and rodents, they return year after year. Whether bulbs are planted in cultivated beds or in a natural situation, we need to remember that many of them originated in the Mediterranean region where it dries out in summer so we should be careful to provide them with good drainage. I saw this to be true with a small planting of miniature narcissus *(N.* 'Tête-à-Tête' and *N.* 'Baby Moon'). They demonstrated their preference for the steep hillside on

FROM LEFT: *Lance-leafed trillium* (trillium lancifolium); *Whip-Poor-Will Flower* (Trillium cernuum); *Great white trillium* (Trillium flexipes); *Trailing Wake Robin* (Trillium decumbens).

Woodhill Road by reproducing dramatically.

When the bulb blooms have faded, it is nice for something to come along to hide the bedraggled foliage and double planting solves this problem. If hostas or ferns are planted in the same beds as the bulbs, they will follow soon after the bulbs have concluded and decorate the same place for the rest of the season. Another perennial following shortly after the bulbs is the variegated Solomon's Seal, *(Polygonatum oderatum* 'Variegatum'). As they poke their heads out of the soil, they look like crochet needles ready for a knitting circle. Vigorous and long-lasting, they provide three seasons of interest.

The spring ephemerals have a short season of gentle sun before the trees leaf out. It is now that the natives display their charm. One of my favorites is the delicate meadow rue *(Thalictrum thalictroides)* as it gently announces spring. Bloodroot *(Sanguinaria canadensis)* leaves protectively wrap the flower until it is ready to be shown. Dog-tooth violet *(Erythronium dens-canis)* has a short life, both in bloom and in return. Later, native spiderwort

CLOCKWISE, FROM TOP LEFT: *Spirea Ogon* (Spireae thunbergii *'Ogon'), is the first spiraea to bloom, sometimes in January, with its tiny white button blooms. The leaves retain a yellow color through the summer and sport a lovely apricot tinge in fall. Maypop* (Podophyllum peltatum) *flowers appear beneath large, sheltering leaves. The blooms last 2-3 weeks and are replaced by a fruit known as may apples. Species Miniature* Narcissus *'Hoop petticoat'; a charming, unusual shaped antique variety.*

OPPOSITE: CLOCKWISE, FROM TOP LEFT: *Fairy Bells* (Disporum flavens) *are a rhizamatomous perennial growing in a slowly creeping clump up to 30" tall in high shade. Blooms in spring with drooping flowers. Bloodroot* (Sanguinaria canadensis). *Miniature columbine* (Aquilegia vulgaris) *is more unusual than the standard version which is promiscuous and an easy mixer. Jack in the Pulpit* (Arisaema triphyllum) *in a typical streamside planting, likes moisture and high shade.*

*(Tradescantia virginiana)* is scorned by some but treasured by others for the electric blue blooms opening successively each day.

One of my spring favorites is native blue phlox *(Phlox divaricata)*. In the right conditions (mixed sunlight under tall trees), it stands up about 12 inches and sports a head of sky blue, faintly fragrant flowers. When spring is over, it obediently tucks itself down to ground level and becomes an inconspicuous evergreen ground cover. A phlox cousin, Jacob's ladder *(Polemonium reptans)*, blooms roughly at the same time in mid-March with lighter blue flowers and is happy along stream sides and moist places.

I have said that I scorn the idea of a "peak season," but when the crabapples *(Malus angustifolia)* and native azaleas *(Rhododendron canescens)* bloom, 2 Beechwood Road is a fairyland for about a week or 10 days, usually at the end of March, occasionally into the first of April. The sweet/sharp scent of the crabapples in their pattern of a Belgian fence is an unexpected surprise and delight, and the delicious scent of the azaleas at the end of the Driveway carries you away.

If we can remember to do so, this is the time to plant zinnias for summer. I usually start them in peat pots so they can be arranged and planted as small sprouted plants when the increasing heat hits the pansies.

## *Summer*

Summer in Alabama is enough to make you get up early in the morning to get your gardening chores done, when it is relatively cool and fresh. We know to cut flowers early in the morning or late in the afternoon so they don't wilt in arrangements. Here, the late afternoon is often not that much cooler than midday because the humidity maintains the elevated heat. When I was a child there was a running contest in the newspaper to guess the hottest time of the day. It was always around 3:00 p.m. The critical aspect with which flowering plants can survive summer

heat is night temperature. If it cools down at night, the plants have a chance to catch their breath, but if it remains in the upper digits, as frequently happens here, they get no chance to cool off.

Sheila Macqueen, the famous English flower arranger with whom I (and countless others) studied, was familiar with our U.S. climates from her many visits. She told me once that she didn't understand how those in the South had the courage or heart to garden here. She was spoiled by her British climate. Rather than sweat and swear about the heat and humidity, we should be thankful that we can enjoy those plants that need varying degrees of heat—Southern magnolia *(Magnolia grandiflora),* oakleaf hydrangea *(Hydrangea quercifolia),* and cotton, including its Malvaceae cousins, Hibiscus and Althea.

Colorful annuals come into their own in summer, creating a splash that, if they are deadheaded, will keep up most of the season. In the big scheme of things, the main reason for plants to bloom is to guarantee reproduction, and if you trick the plant by interrupting this cycle and remove the spent blooms before they

LEFT: *In late spring and early summer, the trees are in fresh leaf alongside the Brook; the purple of the American smoke tree* (Cotinus obovatus) *contrasts with the graphic patterns of the cinnamon ferns and maypop leaves.*

OPPOSITE, TOP: *While this cut-leaf Japanese maple provides great fall color, plus unusual winter sculptural interest, I also enjoy the texture and pattern of its leaves in summer.*

OPPOSITE BELOW, LEFT TO RIGHT: *Snowflake hydrangea* (Hydrangea quercifolia *'Snowflake') has multiple bracted inflourescence. This variety was discovered and promoted by Eddie Aldridge. Black-eyed Susan* (Rudbeckia *'Goldstrum') is an easy, dependable wild flower which likes sun. Meadow rue* (Thalictrum aqilegifolium) *grows tall with feathery flowers.*

can form seed, the plant will go on blooming to perpetuate itself. Some of the summer flowering treats available are Blanket flower *(Gaillardia pulchella),* many colored Cosmos (easy from seed), Gomphrena from red to pink to white, Lantana, with good bloom over a long season, and the many varieties of sunflower *(Helianthus* sp.). *Rudbeckia* sp. offers a variety of daisy-like Black-eyed Susan plants, mostly yellow or orange with a darker center, but there are also some russet tones. All of these are readily available, but they do require sun.

Zinnias and dahlias both provide a multitude of colorful bloom throughout the summer. The dahlias need some winter protection, so I either store them in the basement or garage or leave them in the ground with heavy mulch.

Perennials such as salvias offer different colors and healthy blooms attractive to bees. *(S. farinacea, S. guaranitica, S.* 'Indigo Spires' each produce blue flowers, and grow to 3-5 feet; *S. madrensis* blooms in fall with yellow flowers, to 7'). *Phlox paniculata* can provide sturdy clusters of blooms on stems 3-5 feet. 'David' and 'Mt. Fuji' are both white and are my preferred phlox. I avoid the common magenta like the plague and have to rout out seedlings carrying this strong color. Watch for mildew, and spray with fungicide when necessary.

Herbs are another treat of summer. Useful for flavoring our food, they also can be attractive as a convenient planting near the kitchen door. Many belong to Lamaceae and consequently have the same requirements: perfect drainage, generous sun, and a neutral to alkaline soil.

---

CLOCKWISE FROM LEFT: *The Toad lily* (Tricyrtis hirta) *likes moist streamsides in high shade and grows to 20"-24". Turk's cap lily* (Lilium superbum) *can grow tall (up to 6') but must have sun. Hostas are reliable shade-loving perennials. Most bloom lavender but some are white and fragrant. Sun-loving zinnias are the light-hearted, colorful flowers of summer.*

Many need to be deadheaded like annuals to keep them producing their aromatic and flavorful leaves, so they need a gardener-cook with a disciplinary hand to keep them neat and tidy instead of their preferred, sometimes unruly, appearance. The old English round: "Parsley, sage, rosemary and thyme…" gives us something to start with. All of these are moderate growers, and if we add to them basil *(Ocimum basilicum)* for the tomatoes, marjoram *(Origanum vulgare)* for Italian seasoning, and mint *(Menthe spicata)* for lamb and juleps, you have a good selection. All of these herbs mentioned are available in many cultivars, both as annuals and some perennials. Some think that rosemary, a perennial shrub, loses some quality in its leaf flavor if it grows too old or too large. I have seen healthy hedges of it growing in full sun and assume that the owner's priority is not the flavor of the leaf but the value of the shrub.

*For those with sun and space, summer is the time for lilies. The Asiatics bloom in June and July while the Oriental ones prefer July and August. Providing well-drained soil, adequate sun and moisture, plus regular feedings with complete fertilizer, lily growers are in for a fragrant and stately treat. Lilies come in all colors but blue and purple, and most stand tall on stems from 3 to 7 feet. I am always amazed at the spots that stand up above the surface of the petal like those on Appaloosa horses. The fragrant white Casa Blanca (above) is just one type of Oriental hybrid lily.*

The plants mentioned above all need sun to perform best. Most of my planting area is shaded by tall trees, and I rely on those stalwarts, ferns and hostas, to provide green in the shade.

Like many other categories of plant, hostas come in large, medium, small, variegated, blue-green, yellow-green. They are perennials, which, if properly fed and located in good soil, will multiply and return for many years. Many of the mail-order catalogs have several pages of selections, and they are often available in quantity at the big-box stores. Plants from these mass outlets should not be scorned or looked down upon. Reliable growers supply them as well as your neighborhood nursery. It behooves us to keep up with their delivery, and if you can reach them promptly after they arrive, you can be assured of quality plants.

Where deer are a problem, plant hostas in the same beds as narcissus. After the narcissus finish blooming, the remaining bulb foliage will repel the deer from the emerging hosta shoots. To protect from slugs chewing holes in the hosta leaves, scatter sand or crushed oyster shells on the ground around the plants. The slugs won't expose their sensitive undersides to such rough treatment.

Weather anywhere is unpredictable and changeable. The summer of 2016 brought unceasing rain during the first half, enabling endemic fungal pathogens in the soil to kill many oakleaf hydrangeas. The second half of the summer was marked with unusual heat and drought, leaving me anxious for autumnal changes.

## *Fall*

T. S. Eliot thought April the cruelest month, but I think September is the nadir in my garden. Things are slowing down, and often the lack of rain turns the ground and leaves crisp-dry. Here, the fall beauties do not seem to come into their own until October, and we just have to make do until then. Allen Lacy calls autumn "the neglected season." Many people think that if they can get through summer, their gardening responsibilities are over. But one of the advantages of the fall season is that we get the beginning of cooler and less humid weather. Days begin to shorten, and conditions for working in the garden are better than they have been in months.

As we move into fall, the coneflowers *(Echinacea purpurea)*

TOP: *My favorite pass-along plant is a peach-colored dahlia which I have sadly lost.*

ABOVE: *Surprise lily* (Lycoris radiata). *There's a great sweep of them in the mondo grass as you come up the Driveway.*

RIGHT: *This climbing aster* (Ampelaster caroliniana) *is nearly engulfing the bird house.*

OPPOSITE: *Succulents thrive with minimum water in natural clamshells at the entrance to the Cutting Garden.*

boast a broad range of colors, and gauras, as well as gomphrena in short and tall forms in pink, white, and raspberry, begin their display. At last, the highlights of the fall season appear with the chrysanthemums and asters. Like anything else in horticulture, these are available in large, medium, and miniature varieties. Because we are confronted with mums from the supermarket, we tend to think of them as seasonal potted domes plumped up into half-round spheres bursting with yellows, rusts, and crimsons only good for a couple of weeks. There are a few other, sometimes neglected mums, such as 'Apricot,' that survive year to year in my Cutting Garden and flop in between asters and sedums and sometimes black mondo grass. It is a lovely pale salmon color that is complementary to other colors.

One of the glories of fall are the asters, which take their own sweet time to bloom but the clouds of heavenly bluish-purple that they provide cannot be obtained from anything else. A recent discovery, to me at least, is the climbing *Ampelaster caroliniana.* This aster is a native scandent vine that needs support and does not display its lavender bloom until late October. I have it trained on a copper wire going up to the gutter outside the garage together with a *Clematis lanuginosa* 'Candida' that blooms in spring. This aster is not readily available but is easy to propagate and I keep a supply of rooted cuttings to give to visitors.

Instead of starting from scratch by propagating my own or buying from the nursery, lately I have been potting up some of the perennial plants going out of one season to make room to plant

OPPOSITE: *Falling leaves make wonderful patterns on the reflective surface of the Millstone Fountain. You can even see one of the tall pine trees.*

OPPOSITE AND RIGHT: *Japanese maples* (Acer japonicum) *have brilliant fall color. Fred Spicer gave me this Waterfall Japanese maple* (Acer japonicum *'Waterfall').*

for the next. In fall, these include white garden phlox *(Phlox paniculata)*, Japanese chrysanthemum *(Kalimaris pinnatifida)*, salvia *(Salvia* 'Indigo spires'), and the wild petunia *(Ruellia)*. All can be potted successfully, and if they are provided sharp drainage they can overwinter in a holding bed with no problem. If leaves fall and blanket them, so much the better for insulation. They do need dividing periodically, particularly the phlox, which tends to die out at the middle of the clump.

The swamp sunflowers at the Pond, if given enough sunlight, are a riot of gold in autumn. Each year I promise myself that we will stake those things that need staking before they need it and cut back those things that grow so tall that they needed staking in the first place. Usually I don't get to these chores until past optimum time. The stems have already fallen over sideways and the tips are growing upward, which means that when they are staked, if you don't break the stem, the flower head is facing downward. A good reference for care of perennials recommends early season pruning to create stronger, bushier plants that do not require staking and delay bloom only by a couple of weeks. A good source of achieving this management system is found in *The Well-Tended Perennial Garden* by Tracy DiSabato-Aust.

Another common foot soldier not showing its attraction until fall is *Euonymus americanus.* Much more open and rangy-growing than its European counterpart, which can become a pest, the native one, with its green bark and twigs, is almost invisible until the seed heads open up with the tan-orange capsule revealing bright red seeds, giving it the common name 'Hearts a bustin'. Flower arrangers go crazy over it then–but at no other time. It is a common sight in the woods, particularly along streams.

---

LEFT: *Early morning sun outlines this beech in winter.*

OPPOSITE: *Camellia* (Camellia japonica) *presents all colors of bloom from white to pink to red.*

FAR RIGHT TOP: *Larger camellia* (Camellia reticulata *'Frank Houser') shows large, full rosy red blossoms.*

FAR RIGHT BOTTOM: *Sweet smelling Daphne* (Daphne odorata 'Aureomarginata') *perfumes the whole area around the shrub.*

One of my favorite native shrubs is the stream companion *Itea virginica,* or Virginia Sweetspire. Usually 4-5 feet tall, open in shade, more compact in sun, in late spring their white terminal 2-6" inch white racemes perfume the air. If in sun, the leaves can display a beautiful mahogany-red fall color and remain on the shrub for a long time before they drop. Most think of it as needing moisture, but I have seen it happily growing away from the streams and even making a splendid show in pots on a sunny terrace.

Sometimes we take foliage color for granted in the fall. Many times, we fail to consider the importance of available sun exposure when siting shrubs and trees, but sun is essential for spectacular fall color. Witness a sourwood *(Oxydendron arboreum)* or a Parrotia *(Parrotia persica)* or a plain old hickory *(Carya glabra)* exposed to a good sunny spot, and see their individual colors in all their glory.

## Winter

Serious gardeners are like anthropologists: they look for bones. They don't hesitate to visit gardens in what many would consider the dead "off season"—winter. It is then that the anatomy is most apparent and the layout is made plain, when the distracting splash of color and bloom has disappeared. When outlines, textures, structures, and forms show their true value, they offer a whole new palette of interest to the discerning eye.

Winter is a favored season because the air is crisp and clear. When the leaves fall, we can see deeper into the woods. For some reason, the sycamores never display their white bark in the

LEFT: *Dramatic berry set on deciduous holly* (Ilex verticillata) *remains after leaves fall.*

OPPOSITE: *Light snowfall points up the graceful twigginess of native crabapple* (Malus angustifolia).

summer the way they do in winter. They look like bare skeletons against the dark woods around them. In winter, we can see the shapes of trees. When we see the outline of the tulip poplar, we can understand how it got its name. Other distinctive deciduous silhouettes reveal their identities: sourwoods always seem to be skinny and lean to seek the light; black gums, sassafras, and hickories possess characteristic bark that is easily recognized; hawthorns and crabapples are a mass of thorny twigs preparing to bloom in the spring, even through a light blanket of late snow. Often, we hear someone request an evergreen for "year-round effect." How much more variety and complexity are provided by deciduous trees, which give varying displays in each season. Who can deny the drama of the chalky white bones of the mature sycamore in winter?

In this season, the herbs are in hibernation and the perennials are sulking in the cold, wet ground; the evergreens and deciduous trees are taking their time about announcing spring; the bulbs are impatient and show their tips; and the quince buds swell and shrink, depending on whether it's a warm or cold day. Thank heavens that camellias are prepared with good bud set and need only a few moderate days to put on a wonderful show. So what that some of the early buds are hit by that hard frost? No one could possibly utilize the profusion of bloom they provide. Inside the house, a simple combination of forced quince branches and freshly cut camellias always elicits appreciative remarks from guests. Paper whites from previous years have been set out in the woods after bloom to naturalize on-site.

During winter, while many gardeners are hunkered down, reading and planning rather than doing any actual gardening work, we in the South are prepping for the season to come. Winter in the garden is one of my

TOP: *Lichens create subtle patterns which become more visible on the barks of trees in winter.*

ABOVE: *Surprising shapes of fungus fruiting bodies appear spontaneously in leaf litter.*

OPPOSITE: *Light snowfall on native crabapple* (Malus angustifolia) *reveals the buds preparing for spring.*

favorite times. True, things have slowed down, but that speaks mainly for the plants, not the gardeners. Now is the time to do things, make changes, move shrubs and trees around. When heat forces plants to transpire, there is always a danger when moving and disrupting. When cool weather comes and the plants can slow (but not stop) that transpiration, it is a convenient time to make changes. If you have the time and inclination, the best thing is to root-prune a couple of seasons before the move. The shrub or tree then makes a mass of small feeder roots within the soil surrounding the cut soil which will be the root ball, and the plant has a much better chance of survival than without root-pruning.

During February, several deciduous trees can be recognized at a distance by the subtle haze of color formed by their nascent buds. The willows sport a transparent yellow crown, elms are bronze, and dogwoods with their swelling buds have turned a pinkish gray. The giant red maples' miniscule, garnet bloom gives these trees a rosy halo, and later, in March, their seeds (or double-winged samara) add a new interest as the leaves emerge.

Another winter treat is the display of lichens on trunks and branches. Enjoying a symbiotic relationship between algae and fungi, lichens grow where the air is cold and clean and on the moist (but not necessarily north) side of the tree. It takes a cold and misty winter day to bring out the splendor of their luster and iridescence. Their uses range from the basis of some antibiotics to the source of dye for Harris tweeds. (I was surprised to learn that the one who first established this relationship was Beatrix Potter, when she was not busy with Peter Rabbit.)

One of the most dramatic shows of the fall/winter season is that shown by the berries of deciduous hollies after the leaves have fallen. The most familiar ones are *Ilex decidua* and *Ilex verticillata,* both of which have many cultivars. One of the common names for *I. verticillata* is black alder, which puzzles me because, at least here, they turn a golden yellow, not black, in the fall. They can tolerate wet feet and I love the display of naked red berries reflected along lakesides in the winter. They bloom very late, into May and June, so they need a specific male pollinator blooming at the same time. (If berries are your main concern rather than genetic purity, most hollies can be fertilized with another species' pollen so long as the blooming time is the same, usually sometime in March for the majority of hollies.)

Winter is not all doom and gloom. One hardy soul determined to lift our spirits and bloom with its small yellow flowers during this season is winter jasmine *(Jasminum nudiflorum)*, but my attempts have proved to be more nudum than florum.

While other areas are locked in ice, snow, and freezing temperatures, the South can enjoy the unfolding of another season and savor the hints of approaching spring. Many varieties of narcissus and crocus appear in ordered succession; the quince that began blooming in January continues; the witch

hazels have opened their fragile-looking but tough, crinkly blossoms that perfume the air alongside the fragrant Daphne and the various camellias will produce white, pink, red, and varicolored flowers until April.

Some think of the seasons as metaphors of human life, that spring is a time of birth and newness of life, summer is more mature and full of activity, and fall is a term for mellow thoughts and slowing down. However, if we think of nature as a continuum and not one year or season separated from the next, we realize that winter is not a conclusion like death but a sleep, which, in the grand scheme of things, is a time of preparation to await the new year and the next cycle of growth.

When I began gardening at 2 Beechwood Road, I happened to be reading Katherine White's collection of essays for the *The New Yorker*, entitled *Onward and Upward in the Garden*. In one of the essays, she talks about reaching the age when she can no longer do the kneeling and digging she had been accustomed to and had to rely on someone else to perform those chores while she sat alongside and watched. I thought, "That time will not come for me. I will always be the active garden participant around here." In fact, that time has now come and I rely on

others to do the chores that need doing.

In thinking about it, perhaps the most rewarding times have been when we were putting our mark on the place: establishing the Brook, building the original Cutting Garden, removing the overgrown azaleas from the Stone Circle and deciding what should go in their place, and most thrilling of all, building the Potting Shed. While I used to stay outside and work alongside the gardeners, even doing maintenance chores, now, after all these years, my stamina does not hold up the way it used to. I still make lists of things for them to do, just as I always have done, but I am not as consumed as I once was. In looking at photographs of the place, it is easy to see the changes that have occurred over 35 years, and I am proud that I have had a hand in their development.

My quandary now is: who will take my place? My children live elsewhere and they are not so deeply involved in horticulture as I am. One is an accomplished, prize-winning author, and the other is the mother of two wonderful children and the public affairs director of an outstanding contemporary art site. Should I make sure that this property remains in one piece or let the natural course of events in landlocked Mountain Brook determine that it be subdivided and additional houses built on it? In the back of my mind, thoughts of a Conservation Easement keep recurring. Would it be wise to determine legally that it not be subdivided? Then who would buy it? It's a hard decision. We all know how fragile a garden is after the owner is gone.

Yet, as a gardener, in the middle of these larger, more abstract questions, I can still take delight in the continuous changes unfolding before me each day. And I can be reassured, even temporarily, that I have protected this spot as my special bounty.

ABOVE: *Giant fallen magnolia* (M. macrophylla) *leaves provide texture.*

OPPOSITE: *David Fuqua constructed this unique gate for the entrance to the Pond. A copper turtle shell replaces a real one which was swept away by a Shades Creek flood.*

***In making a wild garden, perhaps the best we can do is to deploy all the discretion and taste we can muster so that our plantings have the air of belonging. Every plant over which the eye can range should look as though it could grow naturally in that place.***

• Russell Page, *The Education of a Gardener* •

# PLANT PROFILES

When I come across an unfamiliar plant (or even a familiar one), if I can learn its family I have a better chance of understanding its needs and therefore placing it in its most appropriate site. Plants within the same family often reflect the same preferences for soil pH, moisture, sun, or shade. When we know that Japanese aucuba *(Aucuba japonica)* is, surprisingly, in the same family as dogwood *(Cornaceae),* we can safely assume that it will perform well in slightly acidic, moderately moist but well-drained soil, rich in organic matter in high shade. The same goes for *Ericaceae,* which includes rhododendron, mountain laurel, blueberries, and sourwood, all of which prefer acidic, humus-rich soil with mixed sun and shade. On the other hand, most of the mint family *(Lamiaceae),* including those culinary herbs with "square stems," prefer alkaline soil, not much water, good drainage, and plenty of sun. An interesting characteristic of most of the buttercup family *(Ranunculaceae),* which, among others, covers clematis, hellebores, and delphinium, is that they prefer cooler temperatures, resent root disturbance, and often contain some toxic properties.

The further we go on our gardening journey, we find that almost every plant that has a history of commercial production has had some nurseryman produce different sizes: big and tall, medium and small. You can usually find one to fit every spot and every season. For us amateurs, it takes constant study to keep up with new developments. And once you learn something and think you have a handle on it, you find that what information you have acquired is just the tip of the iceberg. That is the challenge and fascination of horticulture. We have to keep studying because new selections are constantly being developed and the taxonomists take pleasure in upsetting the family tree and assigning familiar plants to unfamiliar families. Then sometimes they reverse the change.

For me, a helpful reference has been *Landscape Plants for North America, Exclusive of Florida and the Immediate Gulf Coast* by Harrison L. Flint. It provides a wealth of information on size, site requirements, and soil prerequisites in selecting trees and shrubs. It includes particulars on space and time and relation to the human form.

When visitors come to my garden, I offer them a map together with a plant list entitled "Some Plants at 2 Beechwood Road" so we can refer to them and I don't have to spell out the names. On the following pages I have listed some of the plants that I have grown here. Some have survived, some have thrived. Some have failed due to either a natural catastrophe or mistreatment.

For convenience I have listed the family alongside the plant name so we can mentally assign each to its own group and learn which plants are related to each other. Designation of "Native" to any of the plants listed below does not indicate that they are specifically native to the "Ridge and Valley" of Alabama, but that most references list them as native to the Eastern U.S. My list is not meant to be expert or exhaustive. I am just listing some plants I have known with a comment or two about each plant.

***ACER griseum*: PAPERBARK MAPLE (Sapindaceae).** There comes a time when any plant nut just can't stand it if they don't have some special plant that is touted so invitingly in catalogues or magazine articles. *Acer griseum* is one of these. Paperbark maple describes it, but it should be more accurately called shiny-cinnamon-colored-paperbark maple. This feature, of course, shows up best in winter when the leaves are gone. Reputedly it is not as happy in the South, so we don't see too many of them, but mine has grown to about 15′ in 10 years. It matures to a small tree 20-30′ tall.

***A. palmatum:* JAPANESE MAPLE (Aceraceae).** This large group of ornamental deciduous trees comes in all shapes and sizes: small, medium, and tall; weeping, columnar; full leaved or cut leaf. This includes *Acer japonicum*, esp. 'Aconitifolium,' which Michael Dirr calls "one of the most beautiful of all fall coloring shrubs." I have several, some in the ground and some in pots. The one planted by the terrace is multi-trunked and 20′ tall. Some in pots are only 18″.

***A. rubrum:* RED MAPLE (Sapindaceae)** is one of our best native deciduous Southern trees; widespread range, great selection of cultivars, excellent fall color. It should not be looked down upon just because it is common and easy to grow. Can reach 60′ tall. The true Southern red maple has strong genes for heat adaptability. Some of the recent cultivars like 'October Glory' last only about 10 years. *John Glover, Gap Photos Ltd.*

***ACANTHUS mollis:* BEAR'S BREECHES (Acanthaceae)** has been a stumper for me. When we see it in Greece and around the Mediterranean it is usually in sun and happy, but when we put it into Alabama sun, it wilts. This sensitivity is probably due to the northern latitude of its Mediterranean home compared to ours. The large, coarse leaves that are the inspiration for Corinthian capitals and other architectural details give a lot of punch, but they have not proved dependable for me. Place in shade to prevent wilting.

***ACTEA* sp.: BUGBANE (Ranunculaceae).** This mysterious plant, previously called *cimicifuga*, has been moved from one place to another with great frustration, at least to me. Like most of the Ranunculus clan, it likes cool weather better than hot. Over the years, it would gallantly send up its spires to bloom in late summer/fall but because of the heat and drought of late summer the blooms would blast. At last I have put it where its feet will stay continually damp along the new path at the corner behind the native azaleas *(R. canescens)* where there is a good amount of underground water. In seasons with adequate or excess water, it blooms happily.

***ADIANTUM capillus-veneris:* SOUTHERN MAIDENHAIR FERN (Polypodiaceae)** is one of the most graceful plants available, giving us pleasure from March to November. In the hot summer, if it flags and browns in August from drought, just cut it with a string trimmer and give it some water and watch it spring back to life. A hard frost will kill it to the ground, but it will take some cool weather beforehand. Like so many ferns, it likes a neutral soil and a modicum of sun. Just be sure to keep it moist.

***A. pedatum:* NORTHERN MAIDENHAIR FERN (Polypodiaceae),** stand tall to 1′ on its black stipe (stem) and holds its fronds open like a palm. It is both majestic and dramatic. Larry Mellichamp, Ph.D., says, "No garden should be without it." I have it combined with its Southern sister *(Adiantum capillus-veneris)* for a pleasant grouping across the front of the house. Both like neutral soil, so a little dose of lime occasionally is welcome.

***AESCULUS parviflora:* BOTTLEBRUSH BUCKEYE (Hippocastanaceae)** is one of my relatively recent plant discoveries. Native to Alabama, it is a colonizing 6-10′ tall, open, lanky shrub that sports long, very showy white sparkler-like inflorescences in June and turns a lovely gold in autumn. It will eventually form large clumps of coarse foliage like the one on the slope above my pond. Dense in the sun, it opens up in the shade. Also, access to sun produces more buckeyes, which propagate easily if you keep the squirrels away.

***A. pavia:* RED BUCKEYE (Hippocastanaceae)** is a 10-15′ shrub or small tree with vertically held red inflorescences reminiscent of horsechestnut, its larger cousin. Its seed, the buckeye, was thought to be lucky by the Indians. The fresh seed of both Aesculus will sprout quickly when sown if you can keep the squirrels at bay.

***AGARISTA populifolia (syn. Leucothoe populifolia):* FLORIDA LEUCOTHOE (Ericaceae).** It beats me why this most leucothoe-like plant was taken out of this genus, but taxonomists are like that. This arching, native evergreen shrub likes moist soil, starts out medium size but will get to 10-12′ while you're not looking. There is a stand of them near the landing at Woodhill Road that Norman kept telling me to cut back regularly so they would stay dense at the base. Years went by and one day I looked at them having grown so tall, and I cleared out all but the tall stems and made what looks like a child's fort. I can't wait for my grandchildren to play there.

***ALOCASIA amazonica:* ELEPHANT EARS (Araceae).** Evergreen tropical perennial from southeast Asia. Large, arrow-shaped leaves to 15″ or more, course texture, gives tropical effect. Needs damp, rich soil, often coppery or purplish tones. To repeat the dark purple to black color, I have planted it in stone boxes bordering the black mondo grass *(Ophiopogon planiscapus* 'Nigrencens').

***AMELANCHIER arborea:* SERVICEBERRY, SHADBUSH (Rosaceae).** Native small tree bearing clusters of white flowers in spring and blueberry-like fruit in summer. Slow to prove its worth. I keep telling it that this season will be its last if it doesn't perform better, and it does, slightly, each year. Clearing out some trees near the Cutting Garden affords it better sun. It is beginning to be a show-stopper.

***AMPELASTER carolinianus (syn. Aster carolinianus):* CLIMBING ASTER (Asteraceae).** It is a perennial deciduous scandant plant that needs support and waits until late October to cover itself with soft lavender blooms. I discovered this wonderful, unusual native plant only in recent years and have used it in a variety of places. Against the house it climbs up a copper wire alongside a *Clematis lanuginosa* 'Candida,' so the clematis blooms in the spring and the aster in the fall. Other places the aster enjoys are on the stone wall of the potting shed and the split-rail fence on neighboring Woodhill Road. Some people cut the stalks back to bloom like regular asters, but I let mine ramble.

***AQUILEGIA canadensis:* NATIVE COLUMBINE (Ranunculaceae)** is one of my favorite natives with its combined yellow and red flowers. They are reputed to be short-lived perennials, but they breed freely with their mates of other species, so one is never sure what will come up next year. Here in Alabama, we are plagued with leaf miner, which evidently has an unerring ability to find and disfigure the leaves. I have learned that just removing the early leaves marred by this pest and allowing subsequent leaves to emerge will usually solve the problem. Otherwise use systemic insecticide.

***A.c.* 'NANA': MINIATURE NATIVE COLUMBINE (Ranunculaceae),** a charming diminutive with similar red-yellow coloring, perfect for troughs or similar containers. If you have access to seeds, spread between paving rocks for a fascinating natural look for those with eyes to see.

***A. vulgaris:* COMMON COLUMBINE (Ranunculaceae),** this is the plain, old-fashioned, spurred columbine, available in many colors, brought over from Europe with the settlers. What could be more graceful?

***A. v.* 'NORA BARLOW': NORA BARLOW COLUMBINE (Ranunculaceae)** lacks the distinctive spurs found on most Columbine, and its spur-less genes are so powerful that its offspring will produce an attractive, usually double flower but with no spurs. The petal color is usually red to pink with white tips. If you care about the distinctive spurs on your columbine, keep Nora out of your garden. *Howard Rice, Gap Photos Ltd.*

***ARALIA spinosa:* DEVIL'S WALKING STICK (Araliaceae).** Mother used to call this deciduous native Prickly Ash. For years there was one leaning precariously down below the terrace. I could see it from the terrace level, but from my office upstairs, I could look down upon it and truly enjoy its creamy white globs that morphed later into a purple-black infructescence for several months. It seeds prolifically, suckers, and is hard to pull because of all the thorns. Its leaves, which are bi- to tri-pinnately compound, are among the largest leaves: 32"- 64" long.

***ARDISIA japonica:* MARLBERRY (Myrsinaceae).** Handsome, low-growing evergreen ground cover for shade: spreads by rhizomes from which 6-12" branches emerge, producing leathery, dark green leaves; tiny white flowers in spring produce small, bright red, round fruits lasting into winter. It is an attractive and useful plant I have in several places.

***ARISAEMA sikokianum:* JAPANESE JACK-IN-THE-PULPIT (Araceae).** This is one of the most dramatic plants I know, and I once won best in show just because the judges had never seen anything like it. The lower part of a tri-partite green bract (spathe) provides sharp white background for a deep purple stalk (spadix), which is the flower. It is an eye-catcher but short-lived here. I have had it at the base of a giant poplar at the end of the Driveway and sometimes people in cars driving by slowly enough to see it would comment on its drama.

***A. triphyllum:* JACK-IN-THE-PULPIT (Araceae).** One of our standard streamside natives for shade. With imagination, we can see the preacher (spadix) in the pulpit (spathe). It is reputed to have been eaten by the Indians after thorough cooking, but it, like all the Araceae, including *Arum italicum*, contains irritants. In some areas on my Brook it is undisputed gang leader in high shade.

***ARTEMESIA:* 'Powis Castle': POWIS CASTLE ARTEMESIA (Asteraceae).** A perennial grown to 15" tall and wide for aromatic, silvery foliage. What a wonderful filler and color de-fuser! All it requires is excellent drainage and lots of sun. It may need nipping back once or twice during the summer, but what an ally! After our unpredictable summers it is usually exhausted before fall and does not last through winter.

***ARUM italicum:* ITALIAN ARUM (Araceae),** beloved of the flower arrangers and those who treasure something new and green during the winter. This heart-shaped leaf of winter ground cover is wonderful until it, like the splintered brooms of the sorcerer's apprentice, appears everywhere. Beware: The Arum family carries a potent irritant. Once when I was trying to be clever, I gathered the fleshy red seeds and scattered them under a beech tree to make a smashing ground cover. My hands began to burn, and after many washings I called the Poison Control Center. They told me it was toxic; they asked my age, weight, blood pressure, and told me to keep washing until it no longer smarted, or get some over-the-counter cortisone cream. They even called that afternoon to inquire about my state of health.

***ASARUM arifolium:* EVERGREEN GINGER (Aristolochiaceae),** a native ground cover common to our pine-hardwood forests as small clumps of heart-shaped leaves covering the interesting small bloom beneath. Crushed leaves release a pleasant odor. Not connected with edible ginger. I had wanted to create an evergreen ginger ground cover on the slope to Woodhill Road. I was thinking it was a rambler, but learned to my frustration that it is a clumper.

***A. canadense:* DECIDUOUS GINGER (Aristolochiaceae).** For years I fought to keep this aggressive native spreader out of my woods. Then I realized that when I got rid of some ivy I could let it go wild. The velvety fresh leaves unfurling in the spring are most attractive.

***ASCLEPIAS tuberosa:* BUTTERFLY WEED (Asclepiadaceae)** is a native perennial milkweed with clusters of bright orange flowers on 3′ stems. Plant in full sun on poor soil. It is a favored attraction for monarch butterflies. It struggles here because of lack of full sun. *Geoff Kidd, Gap Photos Ltd.*

***ATHYRIUM niponicum var.* 'PICTUM': JAPANESE PAINTED FERN (Athyriaceae)** is another means of getting some light into dark places. It needs some sun, but it gives a variety of gray iridescence along its rachis, or branches.

***BEGONIA grandis:* HARDY BEGONIA (syn. BEGONIA EVANSIANA) (Begoniaceae).** A real trooper in the Southern summer garden. It comes back either where you want it or where you don't but is very easy to remove because it has hardly any root system. As such, it is hard to move once it has come up; best to throw out the seeds and bulblets left on the stalks in the fall wherever you want them to emerge next year. In April they will begin to appear and by July will begin to bloom. They do not need deadheading, and indeed, the tripartite seedheads are attractive. They suffer cutting and arranging in the house with little affront and offer a simple home arrangement, either alone or in concert with other flowers. They like a mix of sun and shade but too much sun scorches them.

***BRUNNERA macrophylla* 'JACK FROST': SIBERIAN BUGLOSS (Boraginaceae)** is a doubly attractive garden perennial to me because of the blue flowers and the nearly white leaves that lighten up the shade near the Pond. It is low growing to 6 inches. But the shade and heat have won, and Jack Frost has lost.

***BUXUS microphylla* 'COMPACTA': KINGSVILLE DWARF BOXWOOD (Buxaceae).** A true miniature boxwood. Plants will eventually grow together for an attractive, matted ground cover 6-8 inches tall in 10 or more years. Russell Page used this massed as flat, fine ground cover. He even clipped it to keep it miniscule; it is one of the few plants that will not outgrow its space in a hurry.

***B. m. koreana*: KOREAN BOXWOOD (Buxaceae).** Boxwood with larger, round, glossy leaves. Takes pruning easily. I have a large pair inside each of my herb beds. I try to keep them trimmed into 3′ balls, and it seems they want more frequent trimming than other boxwood.

***B. sempervirens:* AMERICAN BOXWOOD, COMMON BOXWOOD (Buxaceae).** Steve Bender calls boxwood "the aristocrat of Southern gardens." There are many varieties, some suited to our location better than others. Plant high and do not allow mulch to cover surface roots, which seem to need to breathe. Correct drainage is essential.

**Tip**: Some Japanese hollies *(Ilex crenata)* are often used as substitute for boxwood. It's easy to distinguish between them: Boxwood has opposite leaves, holly has alternate.

***B. s.* 'SUFFRUTICOSA': ENGLISH BOXWOOD (Buxaceae)** is dense, compact, and distinguished by a rounded leaf. Usually used as an edging plant maintained about 1 foot tall. Slow growth will attain 5′to 8′ in 45 to 100 years. Periodic thinning, done correctly, prevents fungal disease in dense growth. They provide the square outlines in my herb garden.

***B. s.* 'ELEGANTISSIMA': VARIEGATED BOXWOOD (Buxaceae),** a dramatic, variegated boxwood with a creamy white leaf margin. Slow growing. Here it marks the corners of the large square parterres of the herb garden. It can be used as an excellent container plant to brighten a shady spot.

***CALADIUM bicolor:* FANCY-LEAFED CALADIUM (Araceae).** A bulb providing a heart-shaped leaf with various colorations growing about 15″ high. At last, we have found it to be a satisfactory summer filler for the voids in the boxwood parterre of the Sunken Garden. 'White Christmas' is one that is mainly white with green veining, giving a cool look in hot weather. We plant them when the ground warms in spring, after the tulips have bloomed, and dig them up in the fall for winter storage.

***CALLICARPA americana:* AMERICAN BEAUTYBERRY (Lamiaceae, formerly Verbenaceae).** Native deciduous shrub to 10′, with arching branches bearing insignificant flowers that turn into dramatic reddish-purple clusters of berries along the stem. One of my mistakes was to think that I wanted to be the only one in the neighborhood with white beautyberry. Not only did I have white berries, but I had trillions of babies. So, they were yanked out and now I have none.

***CALYCANTHUS floridus:* SWEETSHRUB, CAROLINA ALLSPICE (Calycanthaceae).** Another choice deciduous native shrub to 10′ tall with aromatic brown blooms in spring. *C.f.* 'Athens' was discovered in Athens, Georgia, with a chartreuse bloom. Both can get lanky in shade; they need periodic clipping or more sun than I have given them. Fragrance, present only in the afternoon, varies with specimen, so test and purchase while in bloom if possible.

***CAMELLIA japonica:* CAMELLIA (Theaceae).** These evergreens bloom in winter with all shades from white to pink to red with all sorts of flecks in between. Paranoid gardeners cover theirs with plastic sheets at the first sign of frost, and they look like ghosts on their way to a picnic. My feeling is so what if some buds are lost? More will follow. Best planting site seems to be in acidic soil under tall pine trees to provide high shade. The plants themselves come in different shapes and sizes, from shrubs to small trees. It is always educational to go to a camellia show. The local Birmingham Camellia Society hosts a show in Birmingham every February. *Theaceae* includes *Camellia sinensis*, Tea camellia, with dark green leaves from which commercial tea is produced.

***C. sasanqua:* SASANQUA CAMELLIA (Theaceae).** Smaller leaves but the same range of color and size of shrub or small tree. Many of these bloom in fall before regular winter season for *C. japonica*. Some of the *C. sasanquas* are reputed to be hardier than *C. japonica,* for example, 'Cleopatra.' I saw it blooming normally during one of our drastic winters in the 1980s when we had sudden drops of 60 degrees and many plants suffered drastic damage.

***CARDAMINE diphylla (syn. Dentaria):* TOOTHWORT (Brassicaceae)** is one of our unexpected low-growing winter delights; a trifoliate, mottled leaf showing a purple underside and providing a pleasant, natural shade ground cover. After producing a delicate white bloom in spring, it retreats before summer comes and then returns in the fall. Like partridgeberry *(Mitchella repens)*, it resents being transplanted. Only nursery-propagated plants have succeeded here.

***CAREX elata* 'AUREA': GOLDEN SEDGE (Cyperaceae).** Narrow grass-like leaves 4-6" in a bright chartreuse bring color and brightness to shady nooks. Reputed to need constant moisture (it will grow in water), it is tucked in around stone steps above my Millstone Fountain. It seems to keep going in all seasons.

***(Not pictured) C. morrowii expallida* (C.m.'Variegata'): SILVER VARIEGATED JAPANESE SPURGE (Cyperaceae).** Variegated grass-like leaves to 6", good for damp places; brings light into shade. Seems to do better in shade than some other variegated plants that tend to lose their variegation with lack of sun. I have it under the *Edgeworthia* near the Stone Circle.

***CARPINUS caroliniana*: IRONWOOD, AMERICAN HORNBEAM (Betulaceae).** A seldom-appreciated deciduous native tree with attractive, distinctive, muscular-looking bark to 30'; scarlet and orange fall color, abundantly wide growing range. Extremely hard wood used for levers and tool handles. Extremely hardy with a large canopy makes it a good choice for a street tree. Can stand wet and flooding. I have a wonderful specimen leaning over the path by the Brook.

***(Not pictured) CARYA* sp.: HICKORY (Juglandaceae).** A genus of large native deciduous trees growing to 50-60′ or more, source of nuts and good yellow fall color of compound leaves. Extremely hard wood. Needs careful siting because it displays aleopathic (discourages growth of neighboring plants) vibes to those trying to grow in its vicinity. Nuts and bark carry a strong dark brown dye.

***CEPHALANTHUS occidentalis*: BUTTON BUSH (Rubiaceae)** is a happy native deciduous shrub. Grows to 15′ around streams. Its summer bloom of clusters of tiny white flowers hung together resembling a ball hanging from long peduncles in August. Late to leaf out. Wide range of growth. It grows near my pond. *Torie Chugg, Gap Photos Ltd.*

***CEPHALOTAXUS harringtonia* 'PROSTRATA': PROSTRATE JAPANESE PLUM YEW (Cephalotaxaceae)** is an attractive evergreen ground cover and a good substitute for juniper for shade. It is not always correctly labeled. If you want ground-hugging plants, you must eyeball them before purchase. Some are more prostrate than others.

***CERCIDIPHYLLUM japonicum*: KATSURA TREE (Cercidiphyllaceae).** Deciduous tree to 60′, good fall color, winter bloom. What nicer gift from one plant nut to another than a special plant? After Frank Cabot was here for a GCA Members-at-Large meeting in conjunction with a Zone VIII meeting in 1993, he sent me a beautiful multi-trunked specimen. I had only seen it in the entrance courtyard at the Chicago Botanic Garden, and I was thrilled. We have moved it around several times, and I hope it does not outgrow its present space between the basement area and the middle path alongside the reverse curve steps.

***CERCIS canadensis*: AMERICAN REDBUD (Fabaceae).** Considered an understory tree to 15-20′ tall, this sturdy deciduous native announces spring with its brilliant tiny pink blooms marching up and down the stem and branches. It is happy in the shade as well as full sun. Unattractive family characteristic is tell-tale long bean pod hanging from branches later in summer.

***C. c.* 'SILVER CLOUD': SILVER CLOUD REDBUD (Fabaceae: Leguminosae).** It took several years for it to grow into the sun, which brings out its white leaf variegation. From a distance, it gives the impression of a tree covered in white blossoms. This effect lasts all spring and summer.

***C. reniformis* 'ALBA' (Fabaceae).** It is a wonderful version of redbud with white blooms, but with glossy darker green leaves, which grew so enthusiastically by the garage door that it shaded out the left of the pair of crabapples in the Parking Court. The whitebud had to be sacrificed, and the crabapple is now doing splendidly, thank you. Now we have the combination of climbing aster and clematis against the wall to give a vertical shot in spring and fall in place of the whitebud.

***CESTRUM parqui:* CHILEAN OR WILLOW-LEAFED JESSAMINE (Solonaceae)** was introduced to this area by Mary Zahl, a talented garden designer who spent several years in Charleston, South Carolina, as well as Birmingham. It is a vigorous deciduous shrub to 8′ tall that needs to be cut back hard each winter and usually produces clusters of light yellow flowers late summer or early fall, but sometimes it begins blooming in the spring and keeps on until frost. I am told it is poisonous to cattle and can cause contact dermatitis in humans. It is also called "green poison berry" and has become a noxious weed in Australia.

***CHAENOMELES speciosa:* JAPANESE QUINCE (Rosaceae)** is a twiggy, thorny deciduous shrub to 6-10′ tall with late winter blooms ranging from white to pink to coral to red. I am not much for Christmas decorating, so I cut quince early in the holidays and put it in water in the basement to force bloom to be ready to bring out on Christmas afternoon with a fresh, simple, linear arrangement. The blooming branches are fine by themselves, even better mixed with camellias, or other flowers of the season. The naturally-occurring red quince blossom will open white inside if not exposed to the sun. An interesting spare arrangement is one made in late summer from the bare branches with the greenish-yellow fruit attached.

***C. s.* 'CONTORTA': CONTORTED QUINCE (Rosaceae).** Like C. speciosa, but this one is contorted, and everything, including thorns, is twisted. Blooms pale pink in early spring. Makes an interesting accent plant. Mine has remained at about 4′.

***CHIONANTHUS retusus:* CHINESE FRINGE TREE (Oleaceae).** A small usually multi-trunked tree with irregular growth; lately deciduous, generous white fringe-like flowers in spring, dark green leathery leaves; late to turn yellow fall color. No pests. A wonderful plant. Will reach 20′.

***C. virginicus*: GRANCY GRAYBEARD, NATIVE FRINGE TREE (Oleaceae).** Small native deciduous tree to 12-15′ tall with filmy panicles of white feathery bloom in May, tolerant of different soils and air pollution. Just like so many others, it needs some sun. Males have more spectacular, longer racemes of scented flowers; females bear blue fruit if pollinated. If possible, purchase in flower.

***CHRYSANTHEMUM*: 'APRICOT' (Asteraceae).** A sturdy perennial for the fall garden; a gentle pale pink color that blends with others and does not call attention to itself. My only problem is remembering to cut it back until July 4 to keep it bushy. Still it flops, but gracefully.

***CITRUS trifoliata*: (syn. PONCIRUS TRIFOLIATA) TRIFOLIATE ORANGE (Rutaceae).** Lustrous dark green leaves, triangular green stem with prominent thorns, deciduous shrub growing to 15′. Wood is hard and dense; early spring flowers popular with bees and butterflies. Fruit can be used to make unsweet marmalade. Can be used for dense, impenetrable hedge; said to be used around prisons to prevent escape. *Paul Tomlins, Gap Photos, Ltd.*

***CLEMATIS* 'DUCHESS OF EDINBURGH' (Ranunculaceae).** A double white. Before I learned that what we think of as the petals are really sepals, I wondered why mine looked half green and half white. In the *Ranunculaceae* family, these plant parts are interchangeable: The bloom probably couldn't decide whether to be petals or sepals.

***C. armandii:* EVERGREEN CLEMATIS (Ranunculaceae).** A rampant grower with dark green, graceful long leaves once it gets started. I have it planted in the ground but trained to look as if it is originating in cast-iron urns on top of brick piers. It is hard to keep it neatly trimmed and still have white, aromatic blooms in February/March.

***C. florida* 'SEIBOLDII': SIEBOLD CLEMATIS (Ranunculaceae).** One of the most dramatic clematis with white sepals and dark purple anthers. I had it growing through and on top of a boxwood at the garage door where it should get ample sun and root protection, but it is temperamental. It has been pulled up by a well-meaning painter, but luckily it resettled with little resentment. It lasted for over 10 years and then suddenly disappeared.

***C. heracleifolia* (Ranunculaceae).** Not all clematis are climbers. *C. heracleifolia and C. integrifolia* are herbaceous non-climbers, or scandent shrubs, needing someone to lean on in a perennial border. Dave Bevan, *Gap Photos Ltd.*

***C. integrifolia* (Ranunculaceae)** has a good blue clematis-like flower, but *C. heracleifolia* has a cluster of medium lavender, small, sometimes fragrant flowers. Like all clematis, they form fascinating seedheads like little tow-headed boys.

***C. lanuginosa* 'CANDIDA' (Ranunculaceae)** is a cross between *C. lanuginosa* and *C. patens*, resulting in one of the best large-flowered whites. It is a long-lasting plant and a vigorous but not aggressive grower blooming in early summer and sometimes again later.

***C. terniflora* (syn. PANICULATA) (Ranunculaceae).** Pick a name, any name, it has had so many. Sweet Autumn clematis is a constant here in the South. It is nearly as ubiquitous as kudzu, but in late August when it clothes everything in sight with fragrant blooms like a light sprinkling of snow, it is magnificent. I cut it to the ground as soon as it has finished blooming, and still some of those seedheads get around and sprout everywhere.

***CLERYERA japonica*** confused in trade with ***TERNSTROEMIA gymnanthera* (Pentaphylacaceae).** This is one whose mistaken name is much more commonly used than its real one. A serviceable dark evergreen shrub, it grows to 10'. It can be used in many ways, such as hedging and screening. It is denser in sun and produces attractive dark red fruits in fall.

*(Not pictured)* ***CLETHRA alnifolia*: SUMMERSWEET CLETHRA (Clethraceae).** This deciduous native shrub grows to 10' and lives up to its name with its fragrant, erect white spikes in summer. It likes the moist situation of stream sides, so I have it growing around the Pond.

*(Not pictured)* ***CLIFTONIA monophylla*: BLACK TITI, BUCKWHEAT TREE (Cyrillaceae).** Shrub or small tree growing to 15' and native to swamps in the Southeastern United States. Evergreen except in harsh situations where it is semi-deciduous. Blooms in long, white, fragrant racemes in March-April, attracting bees and butterflies. It also enjoys moist, shady streamsides.

***CONSOLIDA ambigua* (DELPHINIUM ajacis): LARKSPUR (Ranunculaceae).** Charming annual, usually in shades of blue. Grows up to 12". Likes medium sun.

***CORNUS angustata*: EVERGREEN DOGWOOD (Cornaceae).** I had this evergreen dogwood on the Brook where it languished because of the shade. We moved it up to the site of the giant poplar at the top of Tornado Alley, where it would get more sun. The first season it appeared to be losing its whole top and I was seriously considering topping it. Luckily, procrastination prevailed and the top leafed out again when it heard about the impending surgery. The second season brought forth a crown of beautiful white bracts as an expression of thanks for the new sun.

**C. capitata: EVERGREEN DOGWOOD, BENTHAM'S CORNEL (Cornaceae)** is hands-down my favorite dogwood. It is evergreen, blooms in June with bracts and fruit similar to *Cornus kousa.* It is not susceptible to the ills common to most of the local dogwoods, so it is the healthiest-looking one I have. It is supposed to be native to the Himalayas but since it does so well here it must be the foothills.

**C. florida: FLOWERING DOGWOOD (Cornaceae).** Small, "edge of the woods" deciduous native tree with creamy white bracts surrounding the true flowers. Grows to 20′ and equally as wide. Many popular cultivars are available, but they lack the graceful, layered growth habit of the true species, which is hard to find now in the commercial trade. For years we have battled dogwood anthracnose, and since it is an airborne fungus, it is hard to treat, even with spraying. We keep looking for a resistant clone, and Tennessesse nurseryman Don Shadow claims he has found it in *C. f.* 'Appalachian Spring.' I have two that have sat and refused to do anything for nearly 20 years.

***(Not pictured)* C.f.'PLENA': DOUBLE-FLOWERING DOGWOOD (Cornaceae).** Imagine twice the number of bracts to double the bloom size. The two here have just proved to be novelty plants in medium sun and have yet to prove their worth. I think more sun would make them happier and they would show off their multiple, showy white bracts.

**C. kousa: KOUSA DOGWOOD (Cornaceae).** Many people have turned to this Oriental beauty as a substitute for the native, but it can be tricky. It demands nearly full sun for good bloom and grows larger and fuller than *C. florida.* It's worth a trip to Longwood Gardens near Philadelphia, Pennsylvania, to see them in bloom in June.

**C. mas: CORNELIAN CHERRY (Cornaceae).** In late winter/early spring the small puff ball yellow blooms on the Cornelian Cherry open before the leaves emerge, and they brighten up the dull days. The exfoliating bark can be very attractive on multi-trunked, mature specimens. A wonderful sight in late February or early March is a clump of *C.mas* underplanted with *Helleborus foetidus.*

***CORYLOPSIS glabrescens*: BUTTERCUP (FRAGRANT) WINTER HAZEL (Hamamelidaceae).** I acquired this plant from Jinksie Burnum (one of the original group of Jeff State students) when my garden club was interested in the witch hazel family. In early March before the leaves emerge, it makes a stunning show with pale yellow racemes dangling from the limbs of a small, graceful, multi-trunked tree.

***CRATAEGUS spathulata*: LITTLEHIP HAWTHORN (Rosaceae).** Jan Midgely, a local wildflower expert, has identified this native hawthorn, several specimens of which have been here as long as I have. It has a wonderful, twiggy, gray-cinnamon exfoliating bark, and the branches sport long, serious thorns. The fragrant white spring blooms produce multiple red fruits in fall, persisting well into winter. An attractive plant for four seasons. Grows to 12-15′.

***CROTON alabamensis*: ALABAMA CROTON (Euphorbiaceae)** is certainly not included in the tiresome ubiquitous plant palette of holly, boxwood, and juniper we are familiar with. It's a rare, native, semi-deciduous (some leaves turn brilliant orange in fall) shrub to 6-8′ with yellow puffball blooms in spring, which morph into exploding seed capsules in early summer. Blanche Dean says it "is one of the rarest shrubs in the United States." It was discovered on limestone river bluffs above the Black Warrior and Cahaba rivers in Alabama, which I would assume would be in full sun. Yet it seems perfectly happy here in our shady, acidic pine woods and produces babies happily. I have found that it tolerates regular, severe clipping, because I have to keep my group at the end of the Driveway cut hard in order to see out.

**CRYPTOMERIA japonica: JAPANESE CRYPTOMERIA (Taxodiaceae).** Oriental coniferous evergreen tree, can grow to 60′ or taller. Needle-like leaves are dark green in growing season, brownish purple in winter. Needs full sun, and makes an excellent barrier or hedge. During our horrendous drought of 2016, this, like *Magnolia grandiflora,* suffered and died in droves.
*Richard Bloom, Gap Photos Ltd.*

***CUNNINGHAMIA lanceolata:*** **CHINA FIR, MONKEY PUZZLE TREE (Taxodiaceae).** A towering, dramatic evergreen tree with dark green needled branches. Makes a powerful statement but a disadvantage is that dead branches turn brown and are reluctant to drop. Can reach 80-100′.

***CYCLAMEN hederifolium:*** **NEAPOLITAN CYCLAMEN (Primulaceae).** Many gardeners do not realize that the natural species of florists' cyclamen can be grown outside in many areas of the country. In fall and winter they offer an intriguing mass of heart-shaped leaves, forming a ground-hugging ground cover followed by pink or white blooms held on 4″ stems. They disappear in summer, when they like to be dry. For me, *C. hederofolium* is the easiest of several species to grow. To propagate more plants, I have had better luck with fresh seed from my own plants than I have from commercial sources.

***CYPREPEDIUM calceolus*, var. PUBESCENS: YELLOW LADY'S SLIPPER (Orchidaceae).** An endangered native ground orchid to 12-18″. Grows in rich, moist woods and bogs. The leaves have parallel veins and unusual flowers, made up of brown or green sepals and lateral petals while the showy part is the modified yellow lip in the shape of a pouch or slipper. I acquired mine from an ad in *The Alabama Farmer's Journal* many years ago. Knowing the dependence between the plants' roots and a mycorrhizal soil fungus, I asked the seller to send me some extra soil in which they grew. They grew, but only a few years. Only carefully-nursery-propagated plants should be considered for purchase. They will be very expensive and will probably expire quickly.

***CYRILLA racemiflora:*** **SWAMP CYRILLA, LEATHERWOOD (Cyrillaceae).** The native semi-evergreen shrub grows to 15′ with whorls of fragrant white racemes of showy flowers and contorted, twisted branches. It must have been here on the Brook originally and has now come into its own since we put in the Pond. Blooms in July when not much else is going on. Plant in a natural setting.

***CLEOME (Cleomaceae),*** common annual, known as spider flower. Usually appearing in shades of deep rose to white. In summer grows to 3′ and seeds prolifically. Thorny stems.

**DAHLIA sp. (Asteraceae).** A tuberous rooted perennial native to the mountains of Central America, grows from 15″ to 6′ with tremendous variety of bloom color and shape. They begin blooming mid-summer but are happiest in the cooler weather of early fall. In areas where the ground freezes, tuber should be lifted and stored in a cool basement or garage.

**DELPHINIUM sp. (Ranunculaceae).** A coveted perennial, growing to 3-4′, a long spike covered with blooms in shades of blue, mauve, purple, pink, or white. In the South, we treat them as annuals because they cannot tolerate the heat.

***DANAE racemosa*: ALEXANDRIAN LAUREL** or **POET'S LAUREL (Asparagaceae)** is one of my all-time favorite plants. It is an elegant evergreen shrub/ground cover with small yellow-green blooms in the spring that turn into fat, round orange fruits in the fall. It forms thick mounds about knee high and seems impervious to insects, fungus, drought, and flood. It likes a tolerably moist, organic soil and high shade. Must be cultivated by seed or division. In spring, new shoots look like asparagus. The growing stems last for at least two years and then begin to look a little yellow and ratty, at which time they are just groomed off at the ground. I got my start of this treasure from Fred Galle after he retired as head of Horticulture at Callaway Gardens, a resort in Pine Mountain, Georgia. This plant is slow to get started and does not like pot culture, so the nurserymen are reluctant to bother with it. When it is found, it is shockingly expensive until the customer realizes how much time has gone into its production.

***DAPHNE* *odora*: 'AUREOMARGINATA' (Thymelaeaceae).** Glossy evergreen leaves on a densely growing shrub to about 4-5'.
I was lucky for 25 years in growing this famously finicky plant, but eventually I suffered the same fate as most others. It was fine for years and then suddenly it was dead. I had planted them on gravel to ensure perfect drainage along with things that wanted to be dry in summer: narcissus and cyclamen. When one grew up above the living room window, I made the mistake of selectively pruning it. It sulked and then died. I still have one by the back door that has outgrown its space, but I am terrified to touch it.

***DAPHNIPHYLLUM* *macropodum*: FALSE DAPHNE (Daphniphyllaceae).** A good candidate for baffling plant experts, it looks like a rhododendron/magnolia cross. It is an evergreen, multi-branched tree with whorls of long leaves that droop in cold weather and is used as a street tree in Korea. We needed a pair of something to mark the piers separating the front entrance court from the garage and Parking Court. I remember that we started with a shrub/ tree that looked like a cross between *Pinckneya* and *Poinsettia,* but it croaked with the first frost. We replaced it with this mystery plant that none of us had ever seen before. It has non-showy flowers and non-showy fruit. The problem with planting pairs became evident in just a year or so. In most cases, the conditions of sun, soil, or moisture are never equal, plus the fact that individual plants often perform differently. The one on the left was slow from the beginning and had to be constantly coddled, and the one on the right had to be repeatedly pruned to keep it equal to the size of its mate. The one on the left is now gone, and its place has been filled with a succession of plants, none living up to the importance of the place. Presently we have a young evergreen dogwood there; I'm not sure which species it is.

***DAVIDIA* *involucrata*: DOVE TREE, HANDKERCHIEF TREE (Nyssaceae).** Probably the most spectacular tree that I know. Those I have seen in bloom have mainly been in England, but the one at Winterthur will knock your socks off. It is a deciduous tree to 40' but higher in the wilds of China. The one I have here had grown into a beautifully shaped small tree, but a year ago a tremendous black gum fell and took the top 20' out of it. We topped the *Davidia* which promptly grew new leaders. It will have better sun now and if it blooms, I will have to have a party and invite everyone to witness it. The showy part of the flower is made up of a pair of unequal-size bracts from 3 to 7" looking as if someone had dropped white handkerchiefs all through the tree. What a sight!

***DECUMARIA* *barbara*: CLIMBING HYDRANGEA (Hydrangeaceae).** Native climbing vine that can be used as a ground cover or allowed to climb into trees. I don't often see the flower because of preponderant shade in my woods, but I happened to look up this spring at the right time and high up in a pine tree where it could get some sun it was blooming happily. It is deciduous and rather than coloring red or yellow in the fall, half of the leaves lose their chlorophyll and become a wonderful ivory color. It loves a creekside and to see it in the beech forest edging Watkins branch of Shades Creek along Cahaba Road is a treat in the fall.

***DICHROA* *febrifuga*: EVERGREEN HYDRANGEA (Hydrangeaceae).** Shrub to 3' tall. References call it evergreen but mine is usually deciduous. In the hydrangea family, it blooms blue in the spring and fruits blue in the fall. Norman gave me the first one; we thought it would go well in the woods with its hydrangea cousins. It languished and didn't bloom or fruit. We moved it to the edge of the Cutting Garden next to the columnar holly for better sun. Voila! Blue blooms and blue fruit! Extracts from it are used in Chinese medicine for urinary problems.

***DIGITALIS* *purpurea*: FOXGLOVE (Scrofulariaceae).** Foxglove's fuzzy leaf rosettes and tall spires of bloom give beefy texture in the Cutting Garden. To ensure white blooms, I start them from seeds ordered from responsible sources. They are sown the summer before, planted out in the fall, and by spring they have acquired real substance. They are biennials, so they are discarded after they bloom.

***DIOSPYROS* *virginiana*: COMMON PERSIMMON (Ebenaceae).** Deciduous native tree growing to 20-30', with orange fruit which is edible only after frost. Good fall color. Hardly ever installed, the ones I have seen were naturally occurring (like sassafras).
*Charles Hawes, Gap Photos Ltd.*

***DISPORUM flavens:*** **(Colchicaceae).** Perennial, bulbous plant, looks like a cross between bamboo and Solomon's Seal. Reputedly can get to 10′, but mine tops off at 4′. I cut it back in spring or late winter to see a display of emerging stalks that enclose attractive drooping yellow-green flowers. Black fruits are attractive to wildlife. Oriental version of fairy bells. Good mixed with woodland ferns and other shade lovers. I ordered mine from Heronswood Nursery, now moved to Pennsylvania.

***D. sessile*** **'VARIEGATUM': VARIEGATED FAIRY BELLS (Colchicaceae).** White variegation lightens up a shaded wooded spot. Upright stalk to about 15″ similar to Solomon's Seal. Produces dangling yellow blossoms. Good woodland addition. I should increase this spot on the middle path across from the top of steps to the Pond.

***EDGEWORTHIA chrysantha:*** **PAPERBUSH (Thymelaeaceae).** Deciduous, open growing shrub to 8′, large leaves to 7″ long, blooming on naked stalks in February. Related to Daphne; extremely fragrant clusters of pale yellow flowers. Coarse texture contrasts with that of smaller, finer-textured surrounding plants. No pests or threats. Can take high shade.

***E. papyfera:*** **PAPERBUSH (Thymelaeaceae).** Similar but smaller in blooms and leaves than *E. chrysantha;* good one to perplex plant people. Not often cited in botanical literature.

***ELAEAGNUS pungens:*** **THORNY ELEAGNUS (Elaeagnaceae).** This sprawling evergreen shrub from 6-15′ has become common and weedy but can be a handsome barrier and hedge and is good in flower arrangements for the silvery underside of its leaves. Reverses usual pattern with fragrant blooms in fall and fruit in spring. Easy grower in sun or shade. Frequent seedlings from silvery orange fruit can take over a property if allowed.

***ENKIANTHUS campanulatus:*** **RED VEIN ENKIANTHUS (Ericaceae).** A plant for true connoisseurs. A semi-evergreen ericaceous shrub to 6-8′ larger in colder climes, with familiar, nodding, bell-shaped flowers and good fall color. I received my clump of four when I finished my stint as Chairman of GCA Horticulture Committee. The Committee usually gives the outgoing head a present: a book, a pin, or some remembrance. Weesie Smith, who had been my Vice Chairman for Endangered Species, rounded up a group of four plants to be planted at my new/old place. Only one remains.

***EPIMEDIUM sp.:*** **BARRENWORT (Berberidaceae).** Low-growing, usually evergreen ground cover plants, related to nandina and berberis, so you know they want a dry situation with good drainage and can tolerate shade. Here, they grow about ankle high. Since they will take some shade, I have them in different areas—the big curve in the path down to the Brook and outside the gate on Woodhill Road. For neatness, it's best to cut back the old foliage in late winter to show off the spring blooms and fresh foliage.

***EQUISETUM hyemale:*** **HORSETAIL (Equisetaceae).** Hollow, leafless, slender vertical stems to 4′. A holdover from the age of the dinosaurs. Like ferns, it has no flowers but reproduces from spores. It is a distinctive-looking plant that can be used effectively in certain circumstances but it is an extremely aggressive colonizer and should be used with caution.

***ERIOBOTRYIA japonica:* LOQUAT (Rosaceae).** Small evergreen tree from China. Coarse, textured, dark green leaves with gray-brown tomentum underside. Grows to 15-25′. Can be frost-tender here, but in warmer climes, winter flower panicles can produce edible, pear shaped or oblong, 1-1½″ pomes in spring. Mother used to keep one in a protected spot for her green arrangements in the house. *Pernilla Bergdahl, Gap Photos Ltd.*

***EUONYMUS americanus:* HEARTS-A-BUSTIN', STRAWBERRY BUSH (Celastraceae).** One of those stalwarts that no one notices until fall when the fruits open. It is a deciduous, open-growing native shrub with green stems and twigs. Left to its own devices in the shade, it will grow to 6′–8′ in a very open, even lank manner. Norman says that he has seen it grown in sun and kept clipped to produce a smaller, more compact bush. Insignificant flowers in spring turn in fall to eye-catching, spined capsules that burst open to reveal bright orange seeds—a flower arranger's delight. I used to think that it was impervious to the scale that decimates other *Euonymus* species, but I was wrong. It is just less susceptible. Everything is relative.

***FAGUS grandifolia:* AMERICAN BEECH (Fagaceae).** One of my favorite trees. Deciduous, stately native tree which can grow to 90′ tall but usually smaller. Leaves turn golden in fall, and many remain through the winter in a pleasant, cinnamon brown color. Likes moisture but needs good drainage, so we see it along sloping stream sides. Most dramatic as a specimen when allowed to let limbs sweep to ground, but this usually precludes growing healthy ground cover underneath. Pointed, cigar-shaped buds are a clue to winter identification.

***FATSIA japonica:* JAPANESE FATSIA, JAPANESE ARALIA (Araliaceae).** Tropical-appearing shrub with large (16″) dark green, deeply-lobed evergreen leaves; grows to 8′. Clusters of small white flowers in fall and winter, turning into black fruits. Valuable for adding coarse texture. Remove seed clusters in winter to prevent overpopulation.

***FRANGULA caroliniana:* (syn. RHAMNUS CAROLINIANA) CAROLINA BUCKTHORN (Rhamnaceae).** Native deciduous tree to 15-30′ in the eastern United States. Full sun or partial shade. Understory tree. Bees are attracted to insignificant flowers. Wildlife creatures consume resultant berries.

***FRANKLINIA alatamaha:* FRANKLIN TREE (Theaceae).** Small native deciduous tree now extinct in the wild. Upright, spreading branches, in growth habit similar to *Magnolia virginiana.* Dark green foliage turns orange/red in fall. Bloom is similar to single white camellia with center of yellow stamens, showing in summer. Extremely difficult to grow in the South, easier north of Washington, DC. Some think difficulty is due to endemic soil fungus where cotton was grown. I have killed three and that is my limit. *Carol Drake, Gap Photos Ltd.*

***GORDONIA lasianthus:* LOBLOLLY BAY (Theaceae).** Seldom-seen evergreen, small, native tree growing in acidic, swampy soils of pine lands and bays of Atlantic and coastal plains. It is similar to Franklinia, producing a single camellia-like white flower, and very particular to its site. Even though they should be happy on the Brook, I have only two remaining out of the original seven.

***HALESIA diptera* 'MAGNIFLORA': TWO-WINGED SILVER BELL (Styracaceae).** Native, small deciduous tree, to 20-30′, usually multi-trunked. Similar to more familiar *Halesia carolinina.* Steve Bender says, "[it is] probably the showiest silver bell, has larger flowers and is a more profuse bloomer." I didn't realize how large it would grow and planted it at the base of a water oak *(Quercus nigra)* near the Millstone Fountain. Now, I frequently have to remove limbs to walk the path.

***HAMAMELIS* virginiana: COMMON WITCH HAZEL (Hamamelidaceae).** Small to medium native deciduous tree, usually to around 25′. Open, rather straggly habit. Bark and roots provide the source for witch hazel astringent liniment. Yellow-orange fall color; extremely small, yellow, fragrant flowers need sharp inspection. There are several multi-trunked ones between the middle path and the Brook. They could use more sun.

***HEDERA* helix: ENGLISH IVY *(Araliacea)*.** Common evergreen vine, many cultivars. Leaves lobed until very mature. Uses aerial rootlets to climb almost anything. Tolerates shade. Serves useful functions in many places but it ends up as a wolf in sheep's clothing. Some people think it looks so neat as a green ground cover, but it is the devil to keep out of trees. I have never seen any really good authority categorically say that such coverage will kill trees if allowed to climb up them, but I can't help but think it is not healthy. Think of having a wrap you couldn't get off, that offered shelter to animals and insects and damp, and you can sympathize with the hapless trees. Sometimes, it proves to be too much of a good thing and needs eradication. Cut it with a string trimmer, wait for the new growth to emerge, and give it a careful application of glyphosphate (Roundup®) or other short-acting herbicide. The new, tender spring leaves will absorb the herbicide while it just rolls off the waxy surface of mature leaves. We need to be aware of the on-going studies trying to determine if there is a relationship between glyphosphate and the alarming rise in autism.

***HEDYCHIUM* coronarium: BUTTERFLY LILY, GINGER LILY (Zingiberaceae).** A tropical perennial lily growing coarsely to 6′ tall, producing in late summer a group of wonderfully-scented white bloom resembling a butterfly, one opening each day. Needs sun, water, and fertilizer. Cut back to ground as stem finishes blooming.

*(Not pictured)* ***HELIANTHUS* angustifolius: SWAMP SUNFLOWER, NARROW-LEAFED SUNFLOWER (Asteraceae).** Tall, coarse, native perennial yellow daisy-like flower with brown center. It bloomed well by The Pond at first but now is shaded out. In the beginning, I underplanted them with Camassia, because it is a bulb that also likes wet feet and shows its blue spikes in spring. They don't make the splash that they did when first planted and they enjoyed more sun. The real fall flowers take their own sweet time and don't show their stuff until October. It grows up to 7′ feet, and, if grown by itself, needs some staking or some will fall over. Sometimes I cut them back ahead of time to keep the height down to reasonable levels and to avoid staking.

**HELLEBORUS (Ranunculaceae).** One of the stalwart, old-fashioned "Grandmother plants." All of about 20 species are perennial, evergreen, winter-flowering groundcovers to 15″. They begin blooming in December with Christmas rose *(Helleborus niger)* and proceed into late winter with the easiest and most popular one, the Lenten rose *(Helleborus orientalis)*. Most leaves are dark green and vary in their division into leaflets. A reliable standby for high shade ground covers in neutral soil. Prefer cold climates, dislike root disturbance, and most parts carry irritating properties.

*(Not pictured)* ***HELLEBORUS* argutifolius (syn. *H. lividus corsicus*): CORSICAN HELLEBORE (Ranunculaceae).** Evergreen perennial to 3′. Long lasting chartreuse-colored flowers found single or clustered in February, March. Taller and take more sun than others of their clan.

***HELLEBORUS* foetidus: BEAR'S FOOT HELLEBORE (Ranunculaceae).** Dark, leathery leaves growing to 1½′. Groundcover bearing clusters of light green flowers throughout spring. Shorter-lived than other Hellebores, but leaves a generous sprinkling of babies to carry on. Long-lasting, likes neutral soil, resents root disturbance.

***H. niger*: CHRISTMAS ROSE (Ranunculaceae).** Handsome evergreen ground cover to 1′ with white blooms, one per stem, developing earlier than other Hellebores, usually in January. Not as easy or common in the South as *H. orientalis*.

***HELLEBORUS* orientalis: LENTEN ROSE (Ranunculaceae).** Easiest Hellebore to grow in the South, therefore most commonly seen. Blooms appear in late winter and continue into spring. Colors range from green-white, cream, pink, dark red and cultivars can be found in exotic shades. Like other Ranunculaceae, it resents root disturbance, prefers neutral soil, can take cold weather. Long-lived plant with few problems. Gardeners should be cautious with exposure to sap, which can be irritating to the skin.

***HEXASTYLIS* *shuttleworthii*: SHUTTLEWORTH'S GINGER (Aristolochiaceae).** Native and choice woodland ground cover with a small, evergreen, heart-shaped mottled leaf that is far from vigorous. Curious urn-shaped flowers hide beneath the leaves. Makes intriguing detail or groundcover in high shade. My most successful patch is at Spencer's Bench; perhaps I should increase that grouping.

***H. splendens*: ASIATIC GINGER (Aristolochiaceae).** It lives up to its name. Not a native, but so spectacular that it deserves a place. Heart-shaped, mottled green leaves form attractive ground cover to 7". Close inspection reveals odd, urn-shaped flowers hidden by leaves. Sometimes it is happy, but sometimes suffers a fungal attack with excess rain. Things clear up when the sun comes out again, even though they are in shade.

**HYDRANGEAS** Where shall we start? Previously assigned to *Saxifragaceae*, they are all now in their own family, *Hydrangeaceae. Southern Living Garden Book* lists six main groups:

***H. anomala*, or CLIMBING HYDRANGEA**
***H. arborescens*, or SMOOTH HYDRANGEA,** native to U.S., includes **'ANNABELLE'**
***H. macrophylla*, or FRENCH HYDRANGEA,** includes both mopheads and lace caps.
***H. paniculata* 'GRANDIFLORA', PEEGEE HYDRANGEA**
***H. quercifolia*, OAKLEAF HYDRANGEA,** native to eastern U.S.
***H. serrata*, JAPANESE HYDRANGEA**

In summer/fall, *H. paniculata* is an old standby. One I have discovered in recent years is *H. p. 'Tardiva,'* probably named for its late bloom, which remains attractive through the fall. If *H. paniculatas* are cut back severely in late winter, the blooms that come on next season's new wood are much larger than those on shrubs not pruned. Like all hydrangeas, they like good drainage, and they can take more sun than the oak leaves and some macrophyllas. Eddie Aldridge, the discoverer of a new oakleaf hydrangea he called 'Snowflake,' turned his 30-acre homesite in Hoover, Alabama, into a botanical garden dedicated to Hydrangea. He has taught many people, including me, much about the genus.

Observe the bloom color of some of the mophead hydrangeas, such as ***HYDRANGEA macrophylla* 'NICCO BLUE.'** The color reflects the relative pH of the soil in which they grow: Pink shows the soil is neutral to alkaline, whereas blue reflects acid soil. Colors can be manipulated by adding lime for pink and sulphur for blue. Sometimes we see several colors in the same planting, showing the diversity of chemicals present in the soil.

**HOSTA** Formerly in the Lily family, it now belongs to the *Asparagaceae*. Called Plantain Lily, the ovoid leaves range from miniatures with leaves several inches long to 15" on giants like 'Madame Wu.' There are all sorts of variegation from white and green to different shades of green on the same leaf. Too many choices to list. They are attractive perennials for shade but delicious hors d'oeuvres for underground voles. To prevent the varmints' feasting, plant them in wire cages or incorporate sharp gravel in the soil.

***HOSTA sieboldiana*: 'Elegans': PLANTAIN LILY (Asparagaceae, formerly Liliaceae).** Popular perennial treasured for shade gardening. This dependable genus offers attractive, heart-shaped leaves in all sizes, many shades of green and chartreuse, and multiple variegations. Some people like the green sculpture of the plant more than the spear of flowers. Problems can occur with slugs or hail.

***HYMENOCALLIS occidentalis*: SPIDER LILY (Amaryllidaceae).** Native to wetlands in the Southern United States. A perennial bulb bearing white, spider-like, showy flowers and coarse, strap-like leaves to 3'. It is close kin to the endangered Cahaba lily. *(H. coronaria)*

**HOLLIES (Aquifoliaceae).**

I became interested in the *Aquifoliaceae* or Holly family when our garden club took on a project from The Garden Club of America to design a garden that included plants that had been featured as subjects of past Plant Exchanges. Topics such as plant families, food for the birds, drought-resistant plants, and native plants were covered in our plan, involving many species of Holly, and I realized what a broad-ranging family it is. Only females bear showy fruit or berries, so a male escort is necessary.

***ILEX x altaclarensis* 'CAMELLIIFOLIA': ALTACLARA HOLLY (Aquifoliaceae)** is a slow, low-growing evergreen that I have beside a rank of steps in the front near the Millstone Fountain. It has topped out at about 4'. It is one, like the low-growing hedge holly and the porcupine holly, that unfortunately happens to be male and thus sports no berries.

***(Not pictured) I. amelanchier*: SWAMP HOLLY, SARVIS HOLLY (Aquifoliaceae)** is a seldom seen, deciduous native holly that languished where we had first planted it in dry woods until I realized that it was a swamp holly. After we moved it to a nice place along the Brook and later, The Pond, it was happy. Then it had its top knocked out by a neighbor's falling tree, but it is putting up a new leader and pushing on.

***I. aquifolium*** is the straight **ENGLISH HOLLY.** It is not as common here as the U.S. natives. Many cultivars belong to this species, including the eye-catching variegated Christmas holly *( I. a. 'Argentea marginata').* When the one I had rooted from a cutting (from my friend Sue Kinnear) gave up the ghost, I was grieved. It had occupied a prominent place in the entrance courtyard, I still have a handsome specimen, however, that John McNabb gave me one year for Christmas. It resides just outside the Stone Circle.

***I. aquipernyi* 'SAN JOSE': SAN JOSE HOLLY (Aquifoliaceae)** is a cross between *I. aquifolium* and *I. pernyi.* It shows its parenthood in its relatively small, spiny, dark green leaves and dense growth to 30′. A handsome specimen is planted between the Parking Court and the back door, so it must be kept clipped to below the roofline and off the path. It needs regular pruning. Nesting robins return each year to complicate grooming.

***(Not pictured) I. x attenuata:*** a group of hybrids of ***I. OPACA*** and ***I. CASSINE*** **(Aquifoliaceae).** Probably the most popular offspring is Foster #2, which is often used as a street tree to 30′. We planted one just off the terrace between a large Japanese maple and an opaca holly. It grew tall and lanky and I began to feel claustrophobic because I couldn't look through it enough to see beyond and down to Tornado Alley. Without much agonizing, we cut it down and breathed easier with the more open view. We also took out the sweet shrub that had overgrown the space between the terrace and the path. The other popular *I. attenuatas* are 'East Palatka' and 'Savannah,' both of which we have on the Berm.

***I. cassine:* DAHOON (Aquifoliaceae)** is a small, evergreen, native holly to 20′ tall. My specimen is fairly open-growing, so much so that we topped it a couple of years ago hoping it would thicken up. The main change was a top knot of new growth. The color is not as dark as most of the evergreen hollies. It is thought to be a heavy fruiter, but mine either is a female, or is sulking in the shade, or blooms out of season from the rest of the hollies.

***I. cornuta:* CHINESE HOLLY (Aquifoliaceae)** sprouts easily from berries dropped by birds and must be removed. It is useful as a screening plant to 30′ with extremely sticky points on the leaves and is the ancestor of many cultivars, including the Burfords. They generally sport a generous collection of red berries in late fall. An interesting observation: those hollies with *I. cornuta* genes hold their limbs to the ground into maturity better than most others, particularly *I. attenuatas* and deciduous ones. Some of the Berm hollies are 'Ike Nelson' and 'Lib's Favorite,' both from Tom Dodd and both show *I. cornuta* parentage. (Lib is Mrs. Tom Dodd, Jr. Tom named one of his many cultivars for her.)

***I. decidua:* POSSUMHAW (Aquifoliaceae).** Deciduous small tree, growing to 6-10′ tall. Light gray bark, red berries on female lasting to late winter. Many named cultivars. Late blooming, into May/June, so they need a male pollinator with similar bloom time.

***I. x* 'Emily Brunner': EMILY BRUNNER HOLLY (Aquifoliaceae).** A cross between *I. cornuta* 'Burfordii' and *I. latifolia,* a popular mid-size evergreen holly. Grows to 18′ tall. Generally, produces good fruit set of red berries. On installation, I labelled them the Six Dwarfs, but they grew and opened up. Then sapsuckers got one and girdled it.

***(Not pictured) I.* 'FEROX': (Aquifoliaceae).** An interesting member of this group used to be called Porcupine holly but now it is listed as 'Ferox,' or Hedgehog holly. It has stiff, erect sharp spines along the surface of the dark green leaf, thus the name Porcupine. Small, not growing more than 2′ tall. My specimen must be a male because I have never seen a berry.

***I.* 'HEDGE HOLLY': HEDGE HOLLY , MARYLAND DWARF: (Aquifoliaceae).** A little known dwarf *I. opaca.* My 25-year-old plant I struck from a cutting from my friend and holly enthusiast Sue Kinnear is 18″ high and about 3′ across. It seems to remain the same size, only becoming denser and wider as the years go by. No fruit.

***I. integra:* NEPAL HOLLY (Aquifoliaceae)** sports dark, almost black green leaves, grows to 30′. When we planted the Berm, we got many seedling *I. integras* from Tom Dodd, and many of them must have been males. An interesting one of the lot, however, seemed to make a vertical statement. Norman selected it and put it at the left approach to the Cutting Garden. It has kept the severe columnar shape and hasn't slowed its vertical progress. He keeps telling me to propagate it and I try from time to time to do so.

***I. latifolia:* LUSTERLEAF HOLLY (Aquifoliaceae).** Large evergreen tree, to 30′, dense with large (to 6″) leaves produces coarse texture. heavy fruit set of red berries. Useful in anchoring an evergreen hedge.

***I. opaca:* AMERICAN HOLLY (Aquifoliaceae).** It is a tall, handsome, evergreen tree to 50′ tall; native to Eastern North America. Hundreds of named cultivars. The volunteer seedlings found here during my childhood have matured into stately giants—one at the end of the terrace and one at the edge of the Parking Court.

*(Not pictured)* ***I. pedunculosa:* LONGSTALK HOLLY (Aquifoliaceae).** Evergreen shrub or small tree, very cold-hardy but not so happy here. Its attraction lies in the fruit hanging from long stalks on female plants in the fall. I asked Beaty for several and he provided them. The only problem was that they were all males, so no long stalk berries. They were returned to Landscape Services.

**I. verticillata: WINTERBERRY (Aquifoliaceae).** Deciduous holly that is more open, spreading, and (to me) more graceful than *I. decidua.* and can be recognized by its darker gray bark marked with horizontal scars. Can take damp feet but does not demand it. Providing there is a neighboring male, fruit remaining on female's bare branches after leaves fall in winter makes stunning display.

*(Not pictured)* ***I. v.* 'JIM DANDY', 'RED SPRITE', 'WINTER RED' (Aquifoliaceae).** Male pollinators for *I. decidua* and *I. verticillata* are important because they flower at the same time in very late spring as the other *I. verticillata* females after other hollies have finished blooming.

***I. vomitoria:* YAUPON (Aquifoliaceae).** Evergreen native shrub or small tree. Many cultivars offer a wide range of different sizes. Traditional, translucent red berries, sometimes yellow. form. Tolerates almost any soil or site, including beach and salt spray. Used by American Indians to brew a tea to induce vomiting to cleanse their bodies before battle. Dwarf forms are commonly used as a substitute for boxwood.

***ILLICIUM floridanum:* FLORIDA ANISE (Illiciaceae).** 6-15′ evergreen tree native to Florida and Louisiana. Dark green leaves, most have maroon flowers, some have white. Both bear an unpleasant, fishy scent. One of few shrubs that will maintain density in shade. *Illicium henryi* has a more attractive foliage arrangement but is hard to find.

***IPHEION uniflorum:* SPRING STARFLOWER (Amaryllidaceae).** Charming perennial bulb native to South America with grass-like foliage and star-shaped white to blue bloom. Easy grower. Prefers dry summer.

**IRIS (Iridaceae)** is a large, varied group of many species, offering many colors and shapes. Most bloom in spring or early summer. Leaves are grass-like or sword-like and provide interesting structure for many months of the year, even before and after bloom. They emerge from bullbs or rhizomes, which should be planted on top of the soil, providing excellent drainage.

***IRIS cristata:* DWARF CRESTED IRIS (Iridaceae).** Low-growing, to 6″, ground-covering native iris with mainly light blue bloom. Good addition to spring ephemerals in high shade and rich, moist soil.

***I. germanica* 'BEVERLY SILLS': GERMAN BEARDED IRIS (Iridaceae).** Rhizomatous perennial with handsome blade-shaped straight leaves to 15″ maintaining an elegance even when not in bloom. Pale-apricot color on this beauty named for the opera singer. Wide range of colors in others. Must have sharp drainage; plant on top of soil.

*(Not pictured)* ***I. pallida:* VARIEGATED IRIS (Iridaceae).** Herbaceous perennial with sword-shaped variegated leaves 2-3′. Blooms lavender in late spring in sun to part shade.

***I. pseudacorus:* YELLOW FLAG IRIS (Iridaceae).** Perennial flowering plant with narrow, erect leaves up to 36″; blooms yellow. Prefers wet conditions, even tolerates submersion in water. Can become invasive.

***PSEUDOCYDONIA sinensis:* CHINESE QUINCE (Rosaceae).** A small tree usually only 12-15′ is struggling to escape its espaliered confinement and keeps growing to the roofline.

**I. tectorum: JAPANESE ROOF IRIS (Iridaceae).** Attractive, shiny green foliage provides a handsome ground cover for several months. Blooms usually appear pale blue, but white is available. Needs a half-day of sun.

***(Not pictured) ITEA virginica:* VIRGINIA SWEETSPIRE (Grossulariaceae)** is a native dark green deciduous shrub growing to 4-5′, naturally appearing along stream sides. Good red color in fall if planted in sufficient sun. I have seen it happily exploding its white spires from a pot on a sunny terrace. Like most shrubs, denser in sun, more open in shade.

***(Not pictured)* I.v. 'LITTLE HENRY': LITTLE HENRY VIRGINIA SWEETSPIRE (Grossulariaceae).** More diminutive than *I. virginica* on all counts.

***(Not pictured) JASMINUM nudiflorum:* WINTER JASMINE (Oleaceae).** Winter blooming shrub; small bright yellow flowers bloom on otherwise bare green branches: fountain shaped to 4′ high and 7′ wide. If I had good sun, I would have good success. With all of this shade, I'm out of luck with all nudi, no florum.

***JEFFERSONIA diphylla:* TWINLEAF (Berberidaceae)** named for Thomas Jefferson. Southeastern U.S. native white spring flower resembling that of bloodroot emerges to 8″. As leaves develop, plant becomes handsome 1½′ mound of twin leaves, split in middle. Prefers rich, alkaline soil in high shade. Weesie Smith gave me a clump, but my garden is too acid for it to be happy and it is gone. *Marg Cousens, Gap Photos Ltd.*

***KALMIA latifolia:* MOUNTAIN LAUREL (Ericaceae).** Our area of Alabama is probably the southernmost limit of this handsome *Ericaceous* evergreen, to 8′ after many years. Unusual white blooms with red or pink exterior in late spring. Slow, rangy growth, but can be quite graceful. Displays better growth with adequate sun. State flower of Connecticut. Many selections and sizes.

***LAURUS nobilis:* SWEET BAY (Lauraceae).** The traditional bay leaf essential to Mediterranean cooking. Can be used fresh or dried. It produces dark green evergreen leaves, takes clipping easily, needs sun and good drainage. Can attain 30′. Plant in protected place: subject to cold damage in Birmingham. I have lost 2 in the last few years from freezing.

***LEUCOJUM vernum:* SPRING SNOWFLAKE (Amaryllidaceae).** Early spring bulb with coarse, straplike foliage. White bloom with green dot on lower edge of each petal. A grandmother plant. Best transplanted while in bloom.

***LEUCOTHOE fontanesiana (syn. L. catesbaei):* DROOPING LEUCOTHOE (Ericaceae).** I get this confused with *L. axillaris.* Both are native evergreen, fountain-shaped shrubs with white terminal racemes in spring, growing to 4′. Shows up best if planted in groups.

***L. racemosa:* SWEETBELLS (Ericaceae).** A semi-deciduous to deciduous native shrub to 8'. Mine is one that has been hanging on for about 20 years down by the Brook. Michael Dirr says that it suckers, creating a thicket, but mine has not performed that vigorously. It is deciduous and under my care, it has produced only scanty ericaceous white blossoms. If only I would remember to fertilize it at the right time, it would possibly be happy. Reputed to be good in dry shade.

***LIQUIDAMBAR styraciflua:* AMERICAN SWEETGUM (Hamamelidaceae).** Deciduous, native straight-trunked tree, to 75', five-pointed leaves turn best dependable fall color, often multi-colored on same leaves. Fruit is a trouble-some spiny ball except 'Rotundifolia,' which produces no fruit. Overall a dramatic mature tree. *Lee Avison, Gap Photos Ltd.*

***LIRIODENDRON tulipifera:* TULIP POPLAR (Magnoliaceae).** Large deciduous tree native to Eastern U.S., grows rapidly with a straight trunk to 60'-90'. In the open its canopy develops the profile of a tulip. Straight trunk and terminal buds give a hint that it is in the magnolia family. After 10-12 years, tulip-shaped blooms occur but they are held high up in the tree and are hard to observe. Leaves are first to turn pale gold and to fall in autumn, often beginning in late summer. *Tim Gainey, Gap Photos Ltd.*

***(Not pictured) LIRIOPE spicata:* CREEPING LILYTURF (Liliaceae).** Black-green, grass-like creeping ground cover, grows to 9". Lavender spike bloom in summer. Can be cut in mid-March with mower on high setting. Larger but not as attractive as *Ophiopogon japonicus.*

***LONICERA fragrantissima:* WINTER HONEYSUCKLE (Caprifoliaceae).** Deciduous shrub to 10'; dull green opposite leaves on stiff, arching branches. Small, very fragrant ivory-colored flowers in early spring. Can look ratty without clipping and attention. *Jonathan Buckley, Gap Photos Ltd.*

***(Not pictured) LOROPETALUM chinense:* CHINESE FRINGE (Hamamelidaceae).** Large, tough, evergreen shrub with dark green leaves and white witch hazel like apetalous flowers, grows compactly to 10' or more, takes clipping so it makes a good hedge or individual plant. Red-flowered and red-leaved varieties have taken over the landscape market to the extent that we seldom see the white one any more.

***LYCORIS albiflora:* WHITE SPIDER LILY (Amaryllidaceae).** White version of the more familiar red surprise lily, emerging in early September. Different colors (pink, red, creamy white) develop at different times in late summer, early fall. Some call these "Surprise lilies," others label them "Naked ladies" because they appear on 2' stalks with no foliage to accompany the spectacular terminal bloom heads. Green bulb foliage emerges later in fall and lasts through winter. Can be slow to begin blooming. *Jonathan Buckley, Gap Photos Ltd.*

***LYCORIS radiata:* SPIDER LILY (Amaryllidaceae).** The familiar red spider lily makes a spectacular show in early fall when left to its own devices to seed where it wants. I have left it alone and it marches across the front lawn of Mondo grass. Can bloom as early as August here.

***L. squamigera:* MAGIC LILY, SURPRISE LILY (Amaryllidaceae).** Pink version of the traditional but stalks taller than *L. radiata.* First of the several Lycoris species to appear. Mine usually show up in late July.

***LYSIMACHIA nummularia* 'AUREA': MONEYWORT, CREEPING JENNY (Primulaceae).** Aggressive, extremely flat-growing ground cover, but useful in certain places. Round chartreuse leaves, about the size of a dime; will spill gracefully over walls or pots.

***(Not pictured) L. minutissima:* MINIATURE CREEPING JENNY (Primulaceae).** Extremely tiny dark green leaves will root every time they hit the ground, thereby assuring good coverage between stones. Occasional tiny yellow flowers. Good cover between rocks or in troughs.

**MAGNOLIA *(Magnoliaceae)*.** Most Southerners consider *Magnolia grandiflora* one of our birthrights, but there are many other species, varieties, and cultivars, both evergreen and deciduous, ranging from large and dramatic to smaller and more delicate.

***MAGNOLIA doltsopa* (syn. *MICHELIA doltsopa*): (Magnoliaceae).** Handsome evergreen tree to 35′, dark shiny evergreen leaves on straight trunk to 30′; fragrant white flowers in January are frequently killed by freezing winter temperatures. After seeing a magnificent specimen in Huntington Gardens in California, I had to have one. Mine grows well in a prominent spot behind the fountain but its blooms are often burned by winter frost.

**M. 'ELIZABETH': (Magnoliaceae)** A cross between *M. acuminate* and *M. denudata*. Deciduous tree to 30′. Produces pale yellow flowers in early spring. Developed by Brooklyn Botanic Garden and named for its longtime director, Elizabeth Scholtz. *J.S. Sira, Gap Photos Ltd.*

***M. grandiflora*: SOUTHERN MAGNOLIA (Magnoliaceae).** Giant evergreen tree to 80′ makes a statement in the Southern landscape; coarse, shiny, dark green leaves with brown undersides and large white fragrant flowers in May/June. There are numerous cultivars of this Southern standby that can be utilized in various situations.

***M. g.* 'LITTLE GEM': (Magnoliaceae).** A popular smaller copy of the larger tree. Reputed to grow to 20′ high in 20 years. Mine, which is espaliered against the house, wants to grow above the roof.

***(Not pictured)* *M. insignis* (syn. *MANGLIETIA insignis*): CHINESE MANGLIETIA, RED LOTUS TREE (Magnoliaceae).** Evergreen upright tree to 25′, fragrant pink to red blooms in June.

***M. virginiana*: SWEET BAY MAGNOLIA (Magnoliaceae).** A small, semi-deciduous, graceful, usually multi-trunked tree, growing to 20′ in moist, acidic soil. Can take sun but prefers high shade. White, fragrant 2-3″ bloom in summer.

***(Not pictured)* *M. macrophylla*: BIGLEAF MAGNOLIA (Magnoliaceae).** Native deciduous tree with dramatic presence growing to 50′. Produces the largest leaves (to 15″) and flowers (to 12″ across) of any magnolia. No significant fall color other than silvery undersides of leaves. Can take sun or shade; denser in sun. Extremely coarse texture.

***MAIANTHEMUM racemosum* (syn. *SMILACINA racemosa*): FALSE SOLOMON'S SEAL (Asparagaceae, formerly Liliaceae).** Clump-forming, attractive, native perennial. Distinct from Solomon's seal in that flowers are terminal on Maianthemum, whereas they dangle along the underside of stalk on *Polygonatum*. Easy to grow. Plant in high shade. Leaves turn golden in autumn.

***MALUS angustifolia*: NATIVE CRABAPPLE *(Rosaceae)*.** One of my all-time favorite plants. Practically impossible to find in the nurseries and difficult to propagate. The ones I have were dug from the woods. It is a small tree with irregular growth to 12′. When its masses of pale pink, fragrant blooms open here in late March-early April, it creates a paradise. Even in winter, its rough, gray bark, thorns, and angular growth produce an attractive, twiggy appearance.

***MERTENSIA virginica*: VIRGINIA BLUEBELLS *(Boraginaceae)*.** Coarse, blue-green leaves surround stems of buds, beginning pink then turning blue as the flower opens. Eastern native ephemeral; appears in early spring, dies down before summer.

***MITCHELLA* *repens:* PARTRIDGE BERRY (Rubiaceae).** This native trailer provides year-round evergreen coverage with its delicate, round, shiny leaves. It makes an attractive woodland carpet. It is found from Nova Scotia to Florida under pine/hardwood forests in rich, moist, well-drained soil. In the spring, a double white flower with male dominant parts in one flower and female dominant in the other flower appears. These twin flowers share a single ovary, which, in the fall, produces a single, red, double-eyed fruit persisting through the winter. Some references say that partridge berry can be propagated by cuttings in summer and fall and by divisions in spring and fall. Not transplanted easily. I have found it to be very particular about who moves it and where it is moved. Despite how common it is, I have not been successful in establishing new plantings with any but nursery-propagated plant material. It is intolerant of drought and wants organic, rich, moist, acidic loam.

***MYOSOTIS* *sylvatica:* FORGET-ME-NOT (Boraginaceae).** Can be annual, biennial, or perennial. Low-growing ground cover with sky blue flowers in late spring. Likes damp feet; grew beside and even into The Pond, but then heat and shade took over.

*(Not pictured)* ***MYRICA* *cerifera* (syn. *MORELLA cerifera*): WAX MYRTLE (Myricaceae).** Dark green, small leaved evergreen shrub or small native tree. Growing to about 15′. Deer proof. Many uses, including hedges and screen. Needs sun or part shade. Dense in sun, more open in shade. Female plants produce fruit containing wax used in candlemaking.

***M. pumila:* DWARF WAX MYRTLE (Myricaceae).** Smaller version of above. Versatile uses: tolerates various soils and exposures; stoloniferous, can be used to prevent soil erosion.

**NANDINA *domestica:* 'YELLOW BERRIED FORM', YELLOW BERRIED NANDINA (Berberidaceae).** Generally, neither Nandinas nor Mahonias stand a chance here. I don't like them because they are weedy and common. The stalwart foot soldier found in the South to ubiquity usually bears clusters of red berries, but there is a form with yellow berries. Stems can reach to 10′ and bear evergreen tri-partite leaves lasting for a year. Legginess can be avoided by periodically removing the oldest canes at the ground. I have followed the Japanese custom of planting this outside an important entrance into the house. It has reached 8-10′ beside the kitchen door.

***NEOMARICA* *northiana:* WALKING IRIS (Iridaceae).** Perennial iris-like plant with slender leaves 1-2′ long. After blooming, the weight of the blue-purple spent flower pulls the stalk to the ground where a new plant is formed.

***NEVIUSIA* *alabamensis:* ALABAMA SNOW WREATH (Rosaceae).** Like *Croton alabamensis,* this is considered an endangered native plant, but it grows vigorously in a variety of situations. A seldom-used, twiggy, arching, deciduous shrub to 6′ with apetalous white blooms in the spring and vibrant yellow color in the fall. Use as a spring blooming shrub like spiraea. I have a clump across Woodhill Road behind the split-rail fence in normal soil and high shade.

***NYSSA* *sylvatica:* BLACK GUM (Nyssaceae).** Native deciduous tree grows 30-50′ or more in time: fairly slowly. Dark green glossy leaves turn deep scarlet/mahogany red color in fall. Underused in natural landscape. Make sure it is sited to get adequate sun. With proper placement, it is a stunner. *Sue Heath, Gap Photos Ltd.*

***OPHIOPOGON* *japonicus:* MONDO GRASS (Liliaceae).** Dark, black-green, evergreen, grass-like ground cover to 6″ spreading by underground stolons. Short, blue-lilac flower spike produced in summer. Can be cut in mid-March with mower set on high.

***O. j.* 'NANA': DWARF MONDO GRASS (Liliaceae).** Dark green, curved blades from underground runners; forms a neat mat that never needs mowing. Not as aggressive or as easy to grow as *O. japonicus.* Can take sun or high shade. Summer bloom turns into electric blue fruit. Reputed to be deer resistant.

***O. planiscapus* 'NIGRESCENS': BLACK MONDO GRASS (Liliaceae).** Larger and coarser than *O. japonicus.* Does not make a solid cover but planted closely makes a permanent statement. Blue spike in summer and black fruit. New growth emerges green but soon turns black.

**OSMANTHUS (Oleaceae)**

We all aspire to a fragrant garden and sometimes take it for granted or do not appreciate it when offered. We should all be more creative with our plants. One way is to keep fragrant plants, such as *Viburnum burkwoodii,* any of the Daphnes, and *Osmanthus fragrans,* in pots of a movable size and, when they are sharing their scents, move them by the front door or onto the terrace.

***OSMANTHUS delavayi:* DELAVAY OSMANTHUS (Oleaceae).** Slow growing, medium evergreen shrub to 4-6′. Smaller than other *Osmanthus* but with the largest flowers, occurring in spring rather than fall. I have it at the rear of the Cutting Garden where it is a team player.

***(Not pictured) OSMANTHUS fragrans:* TEA OLIVE, SWEET OLIVE (Oleaceae).** Evergreen shrub to 10′ or more with age, sun to partial shade. It bears inconspicuous but fragrant flowers which open sporadically throughout the fall season. I've always heard that you should plant this fall treasure near the terrace or an entrance to the house so you can enjoy the scent as you pass. Another reason to plant it close is when sudden hard frosts come, it is easier to throw a protective sheet over it if it is growing in a convenient place than if it is on the back forty. Most of the *Osmanthus* tribe have fragrance, but the most distinctive is that of *O. fragrans.* The scent is not overwhelmingly sweet; there is a crispness to it.

***O.f. FORMA aurantiacus:* ORANGE TEA OLIVE (Oleaceae).** Distinct from *O. fragrans* in that clusters of orange flowers emerge in early fall in a blaze of glory for a couple of weeks and do not continue through the season. Sometimes plants will surprise you and defy the rules set up in the references. I planted this tea olive beside the basement door, which is below the Stone Terrace, and I thought the scent would waft up to that level. Little did I know that it would grow past the level of the terrace and it doesn't seem to be slowing down. (Michael Dirr calls the flowers pale orange, but these seem much brighter to me.) Distinct from the straight species, this one seems to bloom all in a burst, and the blooms do not seem to me to be as fragrant as the rest of the species.

***O. fortunei:* FORTUNE'S OSMANTHUS (Oleaceae).** A hybrid between *O. heterophyllus* and *O. fragrans.* A large, dense dark-green evergreen shrub to 20′. Tiny, fragrant white flowers bloom in fall. Very cold hardy, hard to find.

***(Not pictured) O. heterophyllus:* HOLLY OSMANTHUS (Oleaceae).** Evergreen large shrub to 20′. Blooms in autumn with minute, white, fragrant flowers. Most upright of all types. Can be confused with holly. Remember that osmanthus leaves are opposite while ilex leaves are alternate.

***OSMUNDASTRUM cinnamomeum:* CINNAMON FERN (Osmundaceae).** A coarse, tall (to 3-4′), native fern with an upright habit of sterile green fronds. Called cinnamon for the color of fertile fronds containing ripening spores. Likes moist, woodsy environment in high shade.

***OXYDENDRUM arboreum:* SOURWOOD (Ericaceae).** Attractive four-season native deciduous tree to 30′. As a specimen with adequate space, it will present a straight trunk, but in woods where it has to search for the light, its irregular, leaning growth helps identify it as Sourwood. Blooms in summer with drooping clusters of fragrant white flowers. Reported to be difficult to transplant. Spectacular crimson fall color.

***PACHYSANDRA* procumbens: ALLEGHENY SPURGE (Buxaceae).** Native to the Southeastern U.S., 6-12". Dull, blue-green sometimes mottled leaves to 9". Grows vigorously in Delaware and similar environs (U.S.D.A. Zones 6 and 7a). Although it is hanging on here, it must prefer the cooler situation.

***P. terminalis:* JAPANESE PACHYSANDRA (Buxaceae).** Lustrous, evergreen ground cover to 12". Spreads by underground stolons. Loose, white racemes to 6". Can compete with tree roots. Variegated selection less vigorous. Too much sun turns it yellow.

***PAEONIA lactiflora:* 'FESTIVA MAXIMA', FESTIVA MAXIMA PEONY (Paeoniaceae).** Heritage perennial flower previously in Ranunculaceae. 'Festiva Maxima' is white, multi-petalled, with flecks of dark crimson; grows to 2½' and blooms in late spring. Long lived grandmother plant, resents root disturbance. Needs winter chill, so most are not happy in the South. Early blooming singles do best here. A cooperative study of peonies for the South is an ongoing investigation by Birmingham Botanical Gardens and Auburn University.

***Papaver nudicaule:* ICELAND POPPY (Papaveraceae).** Short lived perennial treated here as annual for colorful spring bloom. Colors range from white, yellow, orange, and red. Slender, hairy stems hold silk-like flowers at 1-2". Can be used as a good cut flower. Scatter seeds in fall, or plant nursery stock in spring for short-lived pleasure.

***PARROTIA persica:* PERSIAN PARROTIA (Hamamelidaceae).** Tree to 30' or more, often multi-trunked; mature specimens produce attractive exfoliating bark. Like most of *Hamamelidaceae,* it is deciduous, produces apetalous flowers in winter, and electrifies the scene with late golden color in the fall.

***PARTHENOCISSUS quinquefolia:* VIRGINIA CREEPER, WOODBINE (Vitaceae).** Deciduous vine native to U.S. east of the Mississippi River. Covers ground, fence, trees to 30' or more. Attaches firmly to support, size of which determines extent of vine's growth. Brilliant scarlet color in fall. Often confused with poison ivy *(Taxicodendron radicans).* Virginia creeper has five leaves, whereas poison ivy has three. Remember: "Leaves of three, let it be." Has become a pest in our area.

***PHLOMIS fruticosa:* JERUSALEM SAGE (Lamiaceae).** Gray-green foliage forms a rather dense, coarse, shrubby perennial to 4'. Norman brought me one after one of his travels, and I temporarily stuck it at the base of a pine tree in Tornado Alley. It has been happy to remain there and after about 15 years it now forms a shrubby gray mass, producing yellow blooms in spring. Like all in this family, it needs good drainage and some sun.

***PHLOX divaricata:* BLUE PHLOX, WILD SWEET WILLIAM (Polemoniaceae).** Choice native evergreen perennial to 10". It creeps along the ground until spring, when it stands up to display clusters of slightly fragrant sky-blue flowers. Wonderful when mixed in a high shade woodland setting with ephemerals and bulbs.

**_P. paniculata:_ PERENNIAL PHLOX, SUMMER PHLOX (Polemoniaceae).** Sometimes called garden phlox, growing erect to 3-5′. An old standby in the sunny, summer garden; fragrant, white, pink, sometimes blue flowers. Prone to powdery mildew. 'David' is a white variety reputed to be mildew resistant.

***(Not pictured)* _PHOTINIA fraseri:_ FRASER PHOTINIA, REDTIP (Rosaceae).** Evergreen shrub or small tree to 15′. Selection from Old Fraser's Nursery in Birmingham was so popular in the 1940s for its quick growth and new red tips, it became overplanted in the local area and is now out of vogue. Other species available. It has generally been replaced by *Cleyera japonica* and *Illicium anisatum*.

**_PHYLLOSTACHYS nigra:_ BLACK BAMBOO (Poaceae).** Large, elegant evergreen bamboo native to eastern China, with arching canes. Green at first becoming black/brown at maturity. Grows to 12 to 15′. Narrow green lanceolate leaves to 5″ long. Plant in sun to part shade; soil tolerant. May remain clump-forming in poor soil. Invasive in warm, moist, or favorable condition. I planted two large pots at the top of the path through the hemlocks down to the Brook. The roots quickly escaped through the bottom hole and put up more culms (stems) until they touched above head level at about 8′ and I encouraged them into an arch. Occasional wayward shoots can be managed with cutting at ground level.

**_PIERIS japonica:_ JAPANESE PIERIS (sometimes mistakenly called Andromeda): (Ericaceae).** Fine-to medium-textured evergreen shrub. Slow growing to 8′ in 10 years. Pendulous ericaceous flowers (sometimes red in bud which have been formed previous summer) can be a handy tool for identification. High shade, excellent drainage. Many cultivars. Planting correctly in proper site is key to success.

**_P. j._ 'VARIEGATA NANA': VARIEGATED DWARF PIERIS (Ericaceae).** A smaller, variegated version of *P. japonica:* extremely slow growing. Likes high shade. In the reverse, curved steps I have one planted that seems to have remained the same size for the last few years. Even in shade, it blooms well.

**_P. j._ 'PYGMAEA': PYGMY PIERIS (Ericaceae).** Extremely small in all respects; so delicate it even resembles a dwarf conifer. The fine texture is eye catching but there are few blooms.

**_P. phillyreifolia:_ CLIMBING HEATH, CLIMBING FETTERBUSH (Ericaceae).** Native evergreen *Pieris* can climb without clinging roots, tendrils or thorns, so in its native swampy habitat, it sometimes climbs underneath bark of nearby *Taxodium disticum* and appears many feet above the ground. Alone it remains a small evergreen shrub to about 2′.

**_PINUS taeda:_ LOBLOLLY PINE (Pinaceae).** It is adaptable to various growing conditions; tall, straight, fast-growing pine to 60-80′. Native to Eastern and Gulf Coast states. After 75 years can reach over 100′. Basis of commercial pulpwood plantations in the South, can be harvested every 15 years. They prove to be brittle in infrequent ice storms, so some homeowners forbid them or cut them down.

**_PITTOSPORUM tobira_ 'VARIEGATA': VARIEGATED JAPANESE PITTOSPORUM (Pittosporaceae).** Evergreen shrub to 10-15′; creamy, fragrant, white flowers in spring. Tolerant of coastal conditions. We previously thought we couldn't grow this or gardenia; they were thought to be "Montgomery plants." (Montgomery is 100 miles south of Birmingham.) Either global warming or better plant selection is responsible for their success here now. In past years, when gardenias were wiped out by killing frosts, we would just go down to Sears or Kmart in March and pick the potted specimen most heavily laden with buds.

***PLATANUS* occidentalis: AMERICAN SYCAMORE (Platanaceae).** Large, dramatic, tall native tree frequenting stream sides and moist areas. Handsome, sturdy appearance; large presence; exfoliating bark reveals dramatic white bark underneath, especially in winter. Can reach 100′. Drops spiny seedballs like sweetgum *(Liquidambar styraciflua)*. There is a very large specimen beside the Brook at the Pond.

***PLEIOBLASTUS* auricomus: DWARF YELLOW BAMBOO (Poaceae).** Miniature bamboo growing only to 3′ with yellow leaves sometimes striped with green. Will run but can be controlled with string trimmer.

***PODOCARPUS* macrophyllus var. 'MAKI': CHINESE PODOCARPUS (Podocarpaceae).** Dark evergreen needled tree to 30′; resembles yew in structure but much larger. Can be used for hedge, screen, or specimen. Sun to high shade. Somewhat tender.

***PODOPHYLLUM* peltatum: MAYAPPLE (Berberidaceae).** Native spring wildflower; extremely large, shiny, bright green leaves on stalk to 12″. Nodding white flower beneath leaves later turns into fruit with medicinal uses. Vigorous grower; announces spring in March; disappears in mid-May.

***POLYGONATUM* biflorum: SOLOMON'S SEAL (Convallariaceae, formerly Asparagaceae, formerly Liliaceae).** Favorite native plant with erect arching stems to 3′. Delicate flowers hang below leaves along stem and morph into blue-black balls eaten by wildlife. Prefers rich, well-drained, shady site where it will form colonies from underground rhizomes. Foliage remains attractive until winter.

***(Not pictured)* *P. commutatum:* GIANT SOLOMON'S SEAL (Convallariaceae, formerly Asparagaceae, formerly Liliaceae).** Native herbaceous stoloniferous arching stem to 4-5′, from which bell-like flowers hang and then turn to dark blue-black, round fruits. Root is underground rhizome that produces clumps of handsome foliage.

***P. odoratum var. thunbergii* 'VARIEGATUM': VARIEGATED JAPANESE SOLOMON'S SEAL (Convallarieaceae, formerly Asparagaceae, formerly Liliaceae).** One of my favorites, with attractive appearance nine months of the year. It emerges quickly, blooms in spring, and maintains handsome looks through fall, when it turns a golden color. It is labeled "odoratum," but I have never been aware of a scent.

***PRIMULA* vulgaris: ENGLISH PRIMROSE, COWSLIP (Primulaceae)** (Primulaceae includes Cyclamen). These old English perennials welcome spring with their butter-yellow blooms on a single stalk, with leaves expanding as the season progresses. This is the easiest primula for us to grow here if put in high shade woodland. After I lost those that Mother had planted to heat and shade, my friend Nanieta Cobbs shared the ones she had raised from seed.

***(Not pictured)* *PROSARTES* smithii: FAIRY LANTERN (Liliaceae).** Larger than the usual species; native to Pacific Northwest. Sports arching stems and large, creamy yellow drooping bells followed by orange-red fruit. Useful but not vigorous in our local shady, acid woods.

***PRUNUS* caroliniana: CAROLINA CHERRY LAUREL (Rosaceae).** An evergreen shrub or small tree native to Eastern U.S. Can grow to 40′. Can be used as hedge or specimen plant; tolerates shearing and clipping, sun or part shade. Tends to be brittle in ice or snow. Seeds germinate easily, so can become a pest.

***QUERCUS alba:* WHITE OAK (Fagaceae)** (Fagaceae includes Beech). Majestic, slow-growing, deciduous native tree to 50-80′, long-lived, native to Eastern U.S. Light gray, shaggy irregular bark found on mature trees, round-tipped leaves. One of choicest oaks but seldom planted because of ultimate size. Hard to find in nursery trade. *Washington Post* columnist Henry Mitchell, says, "It is the final summing up of everything splendid in oaks. The only trouble with planting one is that 150 years or 350 years from now, it will break some gardener's heart to see it die."

***Q. nigra*: WATER OAK (Fagaceae).** Growth to 80′; native deciduous tree; drops leaves through the winter, tolerates most soils other than alkaline. Some consider this a "weed tree," but it is useful as a street or shade tree. Continual leaf drop throughout the year can be a maintenance problem.

### RHODODENDRON

All azaleas are rhododendrons and thus members of the *Ericaceae*. I must admit my strong preference for native azaleas over the Asian ones for many reasons: graceful growth, wonderful scent, and appropriateness for woodland. They are called "wild honeysuckle" by some old-timers for the similarity of scents. Most are deciduous except *R. minus*. They should be purchased in flower to be sure of color. Previously we thought of them as shade-loving, but whenever they have been given more sun as (when a tree falls and opens up a space) they have flourished.

***(Not pictured) RHODODENDRON alabamense:* ALABAMA AZALEA (Ericaceae).** Native to Alabama and Georgia; suckers to form colonies. Early, white, fragrant bloom with yellow splotch. Grows to 6′. They are reputed to bloom well even in shade, so I have peppered them into the ivy-covered bank above the Brook.

***R. austrinum:* FLORIDA FLAME AZALEA (Ericaceae).** Native; distinguished from *R. calendulaceum* by producing a glorious scent. Grows 6 -12′. Blooms in spring from yellow, orange, to red; tolerant of heat, humidity, drought. It was labeled by early plantsman explorer naturalist William Bartram in 1791 as "the most gay and brilliant flowering shrub yet known."

***R. canescens:* PIEDMONT AZALEA (Ericaceae).** Native, multi-trunked, open shrub to 12-15′ with age, fragrant bloom; color is usually pink but occasionally white. They traditionally bloom in concert with the crabapples *(Malus angustifolia)* in late March or early April. Thought to be shade lovers, but more sun affords more generous bloom.

***R. prunifolium:* PLUMLEAF AZALEA (Ericaceae).** Native to parts of Georgia and Alabama, blooms scarlet in July/August, can grow to 8-10′, one of latest to bloom. Signature plant of Callaway Gardens.

***R. schlippenbachii:* ROYAL AZALEA (Ericaceae).** The exception to the rule of mainly native azaleas here. It is deciduous, but from the Orient. Michael Dirr's admiring estimation: "No adequate way to do justice to the beauty of this plant by the written word." He also says it is "one of the most delicate and beautiful of the azaleas for northern gardens," which may explain why I have only one left of an original three. Reaches 6-8′ high, same wide. Beautiful pale pink, large blooms in late spring.

***ROHDEA japonica:* LILY OF CHINA, SACRED LILY (Asparagaceae).** Native of eastern Asia, evergreen coarse straplike leaves form central core to 12″. Insignificant flowers morph into showy red berries in fall. Tolerates dry conditions. Magnificent as massed evergreen ground cover for shade.

***ROSA* *banksiae:*** **LADY BANKS'S ROSE (Rosaceae).** Mainly thornless evergreen sprawling climber to 15-20″. Fine dark green leaves. Like all roses, it needs sun. Vigorous grower, blooms usually yellow (sometimes white) in late spring; slight scent. Can be used as ground cover or climber but must be supported. Commonly found in old Southern gardens.

***RUBUS* *calcynoides:*** **CREEPING RASPBERRY (Rosaceae).** Noninvasive, semi-evergreen, flat-growing ground cover bears creamy white flowers in spring and then (edible) orange fruits in summer followed by deep red color in fall. Needs sun to provide complete cover.

***RUDBECKIA* *hirta*** **'GOLDSTURM': BLACK-EYED SUSAN (Asteraceae).** Native summer perennial for sun, grows to 3-4′, yellow ray flowers with black to brown center; forms large clumps. Seeds easily.

***RUSCUS* *hypoglossum:*** **BUTCHER'S BROOM (Asparagaceae).** Very stiff, evergreen, shrub-like plant to 18″. Flat cladodes (shoots) appear as spine-tipped leaves. Tiny white blooms appear in center of dark green cladodes. Females produce red berries if pollinated. Slow growing, dark green foliage plant that can be good for troughs.

***SALVIA*** **'INDIGO SPIRES': INDIGO SPIRES SALVIA (Lamiaceae).** Summer perennial to 4′, needs sun. Spikes of blue-violet flowers bloom July to frost; persistent purple calyxes contribute to floral effect.

***SALVIA* *madrensis:*** **FORSYTHIA SAGE (Lamiaceae)** is a giant, yellow, late-blooming perennial with its square stems 1-2″ across and up to 7′. Long nights in the fall trigger bloom. *Carole Drake, Gap Photos Ltd.*

***SARCOCOCCA* *confusa:*** **SWEET BOX (Buxaceae).** Evergreen, dark glossy green shrub to 7′. Fragrant, small, white, winter bloom. Said to tolerate shade and dry soil, but mine are not as happy as their boxwood cousins.

***S. hookeriana*** **'HUMILIS': HIMALAYAN SWEET BOX (Buxaceae).** Good ground cover to 1′, spreads to 8′ wide by underground runners. Resembles *S. confusa* in color and leaf. I lost a lot of them in the 2016 drought.

***SARRACENIA*** **sp.: PITCHER PLANT (Sarraceniaceae).** Several species of carnivorous plant are native to sunny bogs and infertile swamps in the Eastern and Southern U.S. Their leaves have evolved into a tube to catch insects for food. Needs full sun. Roots need to be constantly wet with clean water.

***SAXIFRAGA stolonifera:* STRAWBERRY BEGONIA (Saxifragaceae).** Neither a strawberry nor a begonia, it is a vigorous ground cover for shade. Leaves are light green with rooting runners like strawberries. In spring, it sports a delicate, vertical stem of small, white flowers.

***SCILLA* sp.: SQUILL, BLUEBELL (Liliaceae).** Spring bulb, grows to 10″, strap-shaped leaves and star-like blue flowers in winter or spring. Usually naturalized among trees and shrubs.

***SELAGINELLA braunii:* ARBORVITAE FERN (Selaginellaceae).** Not a fern but a fern ally. Looks like a dwarf conifer. Forms dense ground cover to 12″ in half sun, half shade. Green in spring and summer, bronze in fall and winter. I have it as a mass planting at the end of the Driveway, and cut previous year's growth just when new growth is beginning to show at ground level in March.

***S. uncinata:* PEACOCK MOSS (Selaginellaceae).** A type of spike moss, 'Rainbow' has a fascinating iridescent blue color when kept in moist shade. Attractive flat ground cover that probably does not permit foot traffic.

***SMILAX smallii:* JACKSON VINE (Liliaceae).** Native evergreen twining vine to 10″ with spines along stem. With its graceful, dark green, shiny leaves, it is wonderful to use as decoration for a wedding or to drape above front door, but it is a real thug when it is growing in the woods and covers the crown of a tree and drinks up all the sunshine. It is thorny and difficult to dig; the main root is a potato-like mass underground. If I think that smilax is a chore, I get the hives when I think about its first cousin, briarvine, or catbriar *(Smilax glauca).* There is no good excuse for this one. With leaves of an ugly opaque green, it is like the ugly stepsister.

***SPIRAEA prunifolia* 'PLENA': BRIDALWREATH SPIREA (Rosaceae).** One of my favorites of spring. Arching, deciduous branches 6-8′ hold clusters of white flowers; blue-green leaves later turn a good apricot color in fall. Michael Dirr has no use for it, but perhaps judicious pruning might satisfy him.

***SPIRAEA thunbergii* 'OGON' (Rosaceae).** Extremely fine-textured, twiggy shrub 3-5′ tall and same wide. First spiraea to bloom in spring, often in January. Excellent golden-orange fall color.

***(Not pictured) STACHYURUS praecox* var. 'MATSUZAKII': (Stachyuraceae).** Deciduous shrub from Japan to 12′ with pendant racemes of flowers, appearing before the leaves in January. Michael Dirr says, "It is considered one of the finest winter flowering shrubs." I rooted one and, even as a small youngster, it sported a graceful inflorescence its first winter. I coddled it and even held up its progress by storing it in the refrigerator for several weeks. My manipulation paid off by winning my only Beattie Medal for an outstanding horticultural exhibit in a GCA Zone Flower Show that April. Perhaps it resented my treatment, though, for it died that summer.

**STEPHANANDRA *incisa* 'CRISPA': CUTLEAF STEPHANANDRA (Rosaceae).** Extremely cut-leaf deciduous mounding shrub to 3′; attractive arching, twiggy growth. Good to spill over banks or walls. Flowers inconspicuous at a distance, interesting close up. Tangerine fall color. Not often seen around here, but I have it in high shade at the Brook next to our new bridge. If it had more sun, it would thicken up.

**STEWARTIA *koreana*: KOREAN STEWARTIA (Theaceae).** Graceful, attractive, small deciduous tree with slow growth to 20′. Steve Bender calls it "an all-season performer." It has fresh leaves in spring, a white camellia-like flower in summer, colorful foliage in fall, and a patchwork of several colors of bark in winter. Mine took 25 years to bloom. Maybe it was frustrated by the fact that in its early days, I tied weights on the lower branches to make them sweep the ground. Now in 2017 it suffered losing one side to a gigantic limb falling from a nearby oak.

***(Not pictured)* STYRAX *americanus*: AMERICAN SNOWBELL (Styracaceae).** Small, open-growing deciduous shrub or small tree to 8′. White, bell-shaped flowers hang from leaf axils in July; later, a drupe forms in August/September. Plant where suspended blooms can be enjoyed from below. Enjoys some sun or high shade.

***(Not pictured)* S. *grandifolius*: BIGLEAF SNOWBELL (Styracaceae).** Native deciduous shrub found along stream sides from Virginia to Georgia; can grow to 12′. White fragrant flowers in May/June in nodding racemes. Hard to find in nurseries.

***S. japonicus*: JAPANESE SNOWBELL (Styracaceae).** Graceful small tree to 30′ with white, fragrant flowers in May/June. No trouble from pests. Should be planted so that hanging flowers can be appreciated by looking up into them.

***S. obassia*: FRAGRANT SNOWBELL (Styracaceae).** Deciduous shrub or small tree to 30′. Leaves larger, rounder than other *Styrax*. White, fragrant flowers appear in long, drooping racemes in April. Plant sun to high shade.
*Jerry Harpur, Gap Photos Ltd.*

**SYMPLOCOS *tinctoria*: HORSE SUGAR, COMMON SWEET LEAF (Symplocaceae).** Native shrub or semi-deciduous tree 25-30′. Appears around stream sides; stoloniferous; flowers are yellow puffballs on old wood, usually not appearing except high up where crown is exposed to sun. Interesting gall appears in spring but does not seem to damage plant.

***Thalictrum* sp. (Ranunculaceae).** There are 24 species in this genus of airy and delicate perennial plants with a tremendous range of sizes, from tiny *T. kiusianum* (to 3″) to *T. minus* (12-24″) to *T. speciocissimum* (5-6′). Leaves resemble a cross between columbine and Southern maidenhair fern and usually are an attractive blue-green color. They bloom in spring in colors ranging from the usual mauve to cream or yellow. If they look tired in summer, a harsh foliage cut and a drink of water will often stimulate fresh foliage to appear.

***(Not pictured)* T. *kiusianum*: DWARF MEADOW RUE (Ranunculaceae).** One of my favorites that, despite many attempts, I have not been able to keep alive. It is an attractive, diminutive thalictrum specimen or ground cover growing only 1½″ and spreading somewhat if happy. My fatal mistake was seeing it successfully grown in Connecticut as a ground cover in a rock garden. Some things are lusted for but unattainable.

***T.minus* 'ADIANTIFOLIUM': FERNLEAF MEADOW RUE, DWARF MEADOW RUE, LESSER MEADOW RUE: (Ranunculaceae).** Herbaceous perennial growing to 3′. Allan Armitage calls it "one of the prettiest and showiest of the meadow rues," and "best for the South." Flowers are apetalous, giving them a semi-transparent look.

***(Not pictured)* Tiarella cordifolia: ALLEGHENY FOAMFLOWER (Saxifragaceae).** Native, clump-forming, low-growing ground cover perennial for shade, with phlox, Solomon's Seal, or ferns. Small flowers in a loose cluster are held on a slender, erect stem. Foliage is evergreen and available in several colors.

***(Not pictured)* TILIA *americana*: AMERICAN LINDEN (Malvaceae, formerly Tiliaceae).** A deciduous tree, native to Eastern and Central North America. Straight trunk to 60-80′ and 30-50′ wide. Size precludes landscape use in most sites. Other species, *T. cordata* and *T. tomentosa*, are used in England and Europe as street and park trees. Not a common tree in our area, but I have one naturally occurring on the middle path leading toThe Pond.

***TRACHELOSPERMUM jasminoides:* CONFEDERATE JASMINE (Apocynaceae).** Evergreen twining vine can be used on support or as a ground cover; adaptable to a variety of conditions, usually likes high shade and well-drained soil. Vigorous grower with fragrant, ivory, star-shaped jasmine flowers in spring.

***TRICYRTIS hirta:* TOAD LILY (Liliaceae).** With its arching, unbranched stalks, it is a little like Solomon's Seal but with terminal blooms and much showier. In fact, the blooms look like little purple orchids. In September, it blooms at the bottom of the hill below the Cutting Garden near the Brook.

***TRILLIUM* sp. (Melanthiaceae, formerly Liliaceae).** Easy to identify—everything in threes: three leaves, three petals, three stamens. Two types: Pedicellate—flower supported on pedicel (stem) above the leaves; and Sessile—flower resting on leaves without pedicel. They are at home in mixed pine and hardwood forests east of the Mississippi and in some of the extreme West, as well as the Orient. With one flower per stem, they announce spring in natural acidic woodland leaf litter.

***TRILLIUM lancifolium:* LANCE-LEAFED TRILLIUM (Melanthiaceae, formerly Liliaceae).** Leaves and flowers are distinctly narrower than other trillium. Stems are proportionately tall in relation to leaves. Freely growing, producing colonies.

***T. luteum:* YELLOW TRILLIUM (Melanthiaceae, formerly Liliaceae).** Sessile, erect stalk to 12″. Similar to *T. cuneatum* except that flower is yellow.

***T. catesbaei:* CATESBY'S TRILLIUM (Melanthiaceae, formerly Liliaceae).** Delicate but showy flower nodding under leaves on tall stalk. Opens white but turns pink with age. Named for artist/ naturalist Marc Catesby, who explored and drew the flora and fauna of the Southeast U.S. 100 years before Audubon.

***T. cuneatum:* WHIP-POOR-WILL FLOWER,** or **SWEET BETSY (Melanthiaceae, formerly Liliaceae).** Largest of Eastern sessile trilliums (1 -1½″). Flower is predominately dark purple-brown but color ranges can be diverse, even yellow. Mottled green leaves. Blooms early March in Alabama. Most prevalent species here.

***T. decumbens:* (sessile) TRAILING WAKE ROBIN (Melanthiaceae, formerly Liliaceae).** Appears to grow flat on the ground, but its stem rests flat on the leaf litter. Mottled leaves. Flower is purple-brown, like *T. cuneatum.*

***T. flexipes:* GREAT WHITE TRILLIUM (Melanthiaceae, formerly Liliaceae).** This is one of those "I have to have it" plants. Buyers should be sure of nursery propagation. Armitage calls *T. flexipes* "the epitome of the American wildflower."

***T. pusillum:* DWARFED TRILLIUM (Melanthiaceae, formerly Liliaceae).** Extremely miniature, growing to 4″ with white bloom.

***(Not pictured)* *TSUGA* *canadensis:* CANADIAN HEMLOCK (Pinaceae).** Fine-needled evergreen tree to 35′ with age. Needles arranged flat on each side of stem. Can take clipping; used for specimen or hedges. In recent years, it has been decimated in Eastern states by woolly adelgid. Should be nursed carefully for the first few seasons to avoid drying out.

***T. c.* 'JEDDELOH': WEEPING HEMLOCK (Pinaceae).** Extra dwarf specimen: at least 20 years old, outside in container, weeps over side, about 3-4″ tall.

***(Not pictured) T. caroliniana:* CAROLINA HEMLOCK (Pinaceae).** Dense, fine-needled evergreen tree; needles arranged all around stem. Cannot take heat and humidity of lower South. I was proud to have one here growing for nearly 20 years in the cool area by the Brook, but it declined and died. When we took it out, we discovered that the flare of the trunk was hidden below the soil, indicating that it had been planted too deeply.

***UVULARIA grandiflora:* BIG MERRYBELLS (Colchicaceae, previously Liliaceae).** Large-flowered bellwort. April/May blooming, perennial native plant. Single stalk with perfoliate leaves and yellow bell-shaped pendant flowers to 2′. Tops tend to bend with weight of leaves and flowers. Attractive addition to spring ephemerals in high shade.

***(Not pictured) U. perfoliata:* PERFOLIATE MERRYBELLS (Colchicaceae: previously Liliaceae).** An attractive, native perennial whose stem seems to pierce the leaves. Produces yellow downward-facing flowers in spring. Later blooming, smaller overall (to 20″), and stiffer stalk than *U. grandifolia.*

***VACCINIUM arboreum:* FARKLEBERRY, HUCKLEBERRY (Ericaceae).** Native shrub with attractive irregular growth to 15′. In the South, dark green, leathery leaves are evergreen and turn mahogany red in fall. Small, white, ericaceous flowers in spring are followed by blue or black inedible fruit. Mature specimens have beautiful exfoliating bark, gray to cinnamon brown. Plant in sun or part shade. Grows in wet bottomlands and along creeks but is drought tolerant after established.

***(Not pictured) V. crassifolium* 'WELL'S DELIGHT': CREEPING BLUEBERRY (Ericaceae).** Attractive evergreen creeping blueberry to 5″ and 8′ long. Developed too much acclaim by N.C. State Arboretum. Lasted only a few years here.

***(Not pictured)* V. macrocarpon: AMERICAN CRANBERRY** (Ericaceae). Native creeping evergreen, 3-6″ high. Dark green leaves ¾″ long turn fiery red in winter. Source of edible cranberry. Did not last more than a few years for me.

***VACCINIUM darrowii* 'JOHN BLUE' (Ericaceae).** Diminutive native blueberry, usually 2′ tall, can grow to 5′. Tiny blue green leaves, white flowers in spring producing sweet black berries. Mine stayed at 2′ for 2 years, finally reaching nearly 4′.

***VERONICA peduncularis* 'GEORGIA BLUE': GEORGIA BLUE SPEEDWELL (Plantaginaceae).** Creeping, (rises no more than 2″), evergreen, perennial ground cover blooming with tiny, electric blue flowers in very early spring. Excellent performer. From Republic of Georgia.

*(Not pictured)* ***VIBURNUM plicatum*** **var. TOMENTOSUM: DOUBLEFILE VIBURNUM (Adoxaceae).** Michael Dirr calls it "possibly the most elegant of flowering shrubs." Deciduous small tree 8-10', usually wider than high. Horizontal branching habit resembles native dogwood in tiered appearance of white blooms.

***V. rufidulum:*** **SOUTHERN or RUSTY BLACKHAW VIBURNUM (Adoxaceae).** Shrub to small native tree, 10-20' in garden conditions, taller in wild. Dark green leathery leaves, deciduous. White flower clusters in late spring, leaves turning orange, red, purple in fall. Berries dark blue in fall.

***VINCA major:*** **GREATER PERIWINKLE (Apocynaceae).** Trailing evergreen stems make a handsome ground cover usually with purple flowers in spring. Vigorous grower. Needs sun.

*(Not pictured)* ***V. minor:*** **DWARF PERIWINKLE (Apocynaceae).** Miniature version of *V. major.* Makes a good massed ground cover. White-flowered selection available if you know where to look.

***YUCCA filamentosa:*** **ADAM'S NEEDLE (Asparagaceae).** Native to Southeast. Low, evergreen shrub, leaves stiff, pointed, 2½' long, loose fibers (filaments) at edges. Stem remains at ground level. Blooms late spring on central spike bearing pendulous white flowers.

***Y. f.*** **"GOLDEN SWORD': VARIEGATED ADAM'S NEEDLE (Asparagaceae).** A dramatic variegated version of above. Boldly-striped green-and-creamy yellow sword-like leaves topped by tall, showy spikes of fragrant, ivory-white blooms in early summer. An easily-grown eye-catcher.

*(Not pictured)* ***ZENOBIA pulverulenta:*** **DUSTY ZENOBIA (Ericaceae).** Glaucous green leaves on a medium-height shrub. Bell-shaped, white flowers in spring. It is appealing to me mainly because it is in the *Ericaceae*, but I have been unable to make it happy. It is a native shrub that I have killed only twice, so I can still have another shot at it.

***ZEPHYRANTHES atamasco:*** **RAIN LILY (Amaryllidaceae).** Native, clump-forming, grass-like foliage to 12". White lily-like bloom after rains in spring. Use in natural planting in high shade woodland. Lots of variations available.

***ZINNIA elegans:*** **COMMON ZINNIA (Asteraceae).** Mainly annuals for summer, offering a wide range of shapes and colors of flowers. For continuous bloom, it should be deadheaded as flowers fade. Wide spacing avoids lack of air circulation and fungus diseases. Needs good sun and drainage. I like to start mine in pots so the seeds don't wash downhill. Once established, I stake them in the Cutting Garden.

***Open, O Lord, the eyes of all people to behold thy gracious hand in all thy work, that, rejoicing in thy whole creation, they may honor thee with their substance, and be faithful stewards of thy bounty.***

• *The Book of Common Prayer* •

# ACKNOWLEDGMENTS

*Listen to the Land: The Creation of a Southern Garden* was published by Birmingham Home and Garden in 2017 to enthusiastic response from both Southern gardeners and naturalists outside the South, selling out the first edition.

The Garden Conservancy, a national non-profit organization whose mission is to preserve, share, and celebrate America's gardens and diverse gardening traditions for the education and inspiration of the public, has renewed its focus in recent years on fine gardens in Birmingham, Alabama. I am deeply touched that they should find my garden of interest and selected it to be part of the Suzanne and Frederic Rheinstein Garden Documentary Program. I particularly wish to thank James Brayton Hall, Pamela Governale, David and Michael Udris of Udris Film, Gil Shafer, Camille Butrus, Alan Zeigler, and Kathy Park for supporting this endeavor to commemorate my work. With the endorsement and appreciation of The Garden Conservancy, we now welcome a new edition of the book to coincide with the local re-establishment of The Garden Conservancy's Open Days and the premiere of the documentary featuring my garden.

I am grateful to my friend Robin Karson, Executive Director of The Library of American Landscape History, who introduced the project to Jonathan Lippincott of Design Books. I thank Jonathan for his leap of faith and dedication to fast track this project to publish the updated edition to coincide with these special events.

I wish to express my appreciation to all those who have offered encouragement and constructive criticism during the progress of this project:

Joanna Hurley, HurleyMedia, LLC, provided my first cushion to land on and has served as a touchstone for advice, guidance, and moral support from the outset.

To my readers, most of whom offered valuable suggestions: Cathy Adams, Susan Alison, Allan M. Armitage, Ph.D., Linda Askey, Nancy D'Oench, Charles Gaines, Richard Lighty, Ph.D., John Morrow, Starr Ockenga, Neil Odenwald, Ph.D., Dick and Dana Pigford, Margot Shaw, Sandra Simpson, Nancy Thomas, Beth Motherwell, George Thompson, Beth Maynor Young, and John Wrinkle.

John Floyd and Fred Spicer guided me through the technical Latin of botanical names and changing plant families, as well as provided repeated readings.

Mick Hales, Sylvia Martin, and Beth Young have provided beautiful photographs in both the past and the present.

Thanks to Scott Fuller's graphic talents we gained our first exciting glimpse of what was to come.

John Wilson of Golightly Landscape provided the complicated map of the property.

During the gestation period, Rick Darke, Ken Druse, Darrel Morrison, and Starr Ockenga offered sympathetic advice.

From the beginning, Halley Cotton kept me on track with the variables of the computer, urged me on with the story, and acted as a generally indispensable assistant.

Ron McKinney forced my computer to keep going when it wanted to surrender to this digitally challenged amateur's touch.

I count myself extremely fortunate to be in the hands of *Birmingham Home and Garden*'s editor, Cathy Still McGowin, who remains unflappable in a tight time frame and constantly able to mold seemingly disparate elements of a story into a cohesive whole.

Rebecca Reeves's design talents are nothing short of miraculous. Regina Dunn helped to shepherd the book out into the world.

All along the process, I am indebted to the following team for sharing their talents in the garden with me: John McNabb, Deborah Keith, John Griffin, all led by Norman Kent Johnson and his remarkable expertise and humor.

But the real gems in this generous group have been my daughters, Anne and Margaret. Anne read the manuscript in the beginning and later hopped on board and helped me figure out logistics of production, launch, and distribution, as well as researching missing photographs for the plant profiles. Margaret has used her many talents in writing, editing, and layout to produce something useful for both the gardener and the horticulturally challenged.

# BIBLIOGRAPHY


Armitage, Allan M. *Herbaceous Perennial Plants: A Treatise on Their Identification, Culture and Garden Attributes.* Brentwood, TN: Cool Springs Press, 2008.

Barnes, Don. *Daffodils: for Home, Garden and Show.* Exeter, Devon: David & Charles, 1987.

Bender, Steve. *The* Southern Living *Garden Book.* Birmingham, AL: Oxmoor House, 2004.

Beutler, Linda. *The Plant Lover's Guide to Clematis.* Portland, OR: Timber Press, 2016.

Bir, Richard E. *Growing and Propagating Showy Native Woody Plants.* Chapel Hill, NC: University of North Carolina Press, 1992.

*The Book of Common Prayer.* Cambridge, UK: Cambridge University Press, 2005.

Brickell, Christopher, ed. *The American Horticultural Society A - Z Encyclopedia of Garden Plants.* New York, NY: DK, 1997.

Brown, Claud L., and L. Katherine Kirkman. *Trees of Georgia and Adjacent States.* Portland, OR: Timber Press, 1990.

Cabot, Francis H. *The Greater Perfection: The Story of the Gardens at Les Quatre Vents.* New York, NY: W.W. Norton, 2001.

Cappiello, Paul, and Don Shadow. *Dogwoods: The Genus Cornus.* Portland, OR: Timber Press, 2007.

Case, Frederick W., and Roberta B. Case. *Trilliums.* Portland, OR: Timber Press, 1997.

Chapin, Lois Trigg. *The Southern Gardener's Book of Lists: The Best Plants for All Your Needs, Wants, and Whims.* Dallas, TX: Taylor Publishing, 1994.

Cotner, June. *Garden Blessings: Prose, Poems and Prayers Celebrating the Love of Gardening.* Berkeley, CA: Viva Editions, 2014.

Cullina, William. *The New England Wild Flower Society Guide to Growing and Propagating Wildflowers of the United States and Canada.* New York, NY: Houghton Mifflin Co., 2002.

Culp, David L., and Adam Levine. *The Layered Garden: Design Lessons for Year-Round Beauty from Brandywine Cottage.* Portland, OR: Timber Press, 2015.

Darke, Frederick. *The American Woodland Garden: Capturing the Spirit of the Deciduous Forest.* Portland, OR: Timber Press, 2002.

Darke, Frederick. *The Color Encyclopedia of Ornamental Grasses, Sedges, Rushes, Restios, Cat Tails and Selected Bamboos.* Portland, OR: Timber Press, 2005.

Darke, Frederick, and Mark Griffiths, eds. *The New Royal Horticultural Society Dictionary: Manual of Grasses.* London, UK: Macmillan, 1994.

Dash, Robert. *Notes from Madoo: Making a Garden in the Hamptons.* Boston, MA: Houghton Mifflin, 2000.

Dean, Blanche Evans. *Trees and Shrubs in the Heart of Dixie.* Birmingham, AL: Southern University Press, 1968.

Dean, Blanche Evans. *Trees and Shrubs of the Southeast.* 3rd ed. Birmingham, AL: Birmingham Audubon Society Press, 1988.

Dean, Blanche Evans. *Wildflowers of Alabama and Adjoining States.* Tuscaloosa, AL: University of Alabama Press, 1973.

Deno, Norman C. *Seed Germination, Theory and Practice.* State College, PA: Norman C. Deno, 1993.

Dirr, Michael A. *Hydrangeas for American Gardens.* Portland, OR: Timber Press, 2004.

Dirr, Michael A. *Manual of Woody Landscape Plants: Their Identification, Ornamental Characteristics, Culture, Propagation and Uses.* 5th ed. Champaign, IL: Stipes, 2009.

Dirr, Michael A., and Charles W. Heuser, Jr. *The Reference Manual of Woody Plant Propagation: From Seed to Tissue Culture.* 2nd ed. Cary, NC: Varsity Press, 2006.

DiSabato-Aust, Tracy. *The Well-Tended Perennial Garden.* Portland, OR: Timber Press, 1998.

D'Oench, Nancy, Bonny Martin, and Mick Hales. *Gardens Private & Personal: A Garden Club of America Book.* New York, NY: Abrams, 2008.

Druse, Kenneth. *The Collector's Garden.* New York, NY: Clarkson N. Potter, 1996.

Druse, Kenneth. *Making More Plants.* New York, NY: Clarkson N. Potter, 2000.

Druse, Kenneth. *The Natural Garden.* New York, NY: Clarkson N. Potter, 1989.

Druse, Kenneth, and Ellen Hoverkamp. *Natural Companions: The Garden Lover's Guide to Plant Combinations.* New York, NY: Stewart, Tabori & Chang, 2012.

Druse, Kenneth, and Margaret Roach. *The Natural Habitat Garden.* New York, NY: Clarkson N. Potter, 1994.

Elias, Thomas S. *The Complete Trees of North America: Field Guide and Natural History.* New York, NY: Gramercy, 1987.

Emerson, Ralph Waldo. *Nature.* CreateSpace, 2012.

Fish, Margery. *We Made a Garden.* London, UK: Faber & Faber, 1956.

Flint, Harrison L., and Jenny M. Lyverse. *Landscape Plants for Eastern North America, Exclusive of Florida and the Immediate Gulf Coast.* 2nd ed. New York, NY: John Wiley & Sons, 1997.

Foote, Leonard E., and Samuel B. Jones. *Native Shrubs and Woody Vines of the Southeast: Landscape Uses and Identification.* Portland, OR: Timber Press, 1989.

Foster, H. Lincoln, Laura Louise Foster, and Norman Singer. *Cuttings from a Rock Garden: Plant Portraits and Other Essays.* Englewood Cliffs, NJ: Prentice-Hall, 1997.

Fox, Derek. *Growing Lilies.* North Pomfret, Vermont: Christopher Helm, 1985.

Galle, Fred C. *Azaleas.* Portland, OR: Timber Press, 1987.

Galle, Fred C. *Hollies.* Portland, OR: Timber Press, 1997.

Godfrey, Robert K., and Melanie Darst. *Trees, Shrubs and Woody Vines of Northern Florida and Adjacent Georgia and Alabama.* Athens, GA: University of Georgia Press, 1988.

Goodwin, Nancy. *Montrose: Life in a Garden.* Durham, NC: Duke University Press, 2005.

Grey-Wilson, Christopher, and Mary Grierson. *The Genus Cyclamen.* Kew, UK: Royal Botanic Gardens, 1988.

Griffiths, Mark. *The New Royal Horticultural Society Dictionary of Gardening.* London, UK: Macmillan, 1994.

Haltom, Susan, Jane Roy Brown, and Langdon Clay. *One Writer's Garden: Eudora Welty's Home Place.* Jackson, MS: University Press of Mississippi, 2011.

Harper, Pamela, and Frederick McGourty. *Perennials, How to Select, Grow and Enjoy.* Los Angeles, CA: HP Books, 1982.

Hastings, Don. *Gardening in the South: Trees, Shrubs and Lawns.* Dallas, TX: Taylor Publishing, 1987.

Henderson, Edith. *Edith Henderson's Home Landscape Companion.* Atlanta, GA: Peachtree Publishers, 1993.

Hipps, Carol Bishop. *In a Southern Garden: Twelve Months of Plants and Observations.* New York, NY: Macmillan, 1994.

Hume, Harold H. *Camellias in America.* Harrisburg, PA: McFarland Company, 1946.

Hume, Harold H. *Camellias: Kinds and Culture.* New York, NY: Macmillan, 1951.

Hume, Harold H. *Gardening in the Lower South.* New York, NY: Macmillan, 1929.

Hume, Harold H. *Hollies.* New York, NY: Macmillan, 1953.

Jekyll, Gertrude. *Home and Garden: Notes and Thoughts, Practical and Critical, of a Worker in Both.* Cambridge, UK: Cambridge University Press, 2011.

Jekyll, Gertrude. *On Gardening.* New York, NY: Scribners, 1964.

Johnson, Norman Kent, and Beth Maynor. *Everyday Flowers: Growing, Arranging, and Living with Your Flowers.* Atlanta, GA: Longstreet Press, 1990.

Lacy, Allen. *The Garden in Autumn.* New York, NY: Henry Holt and Company, 1990.

Lacy, Allen. *The Inviting Garden: Gardening for the Senses, Mind, and Spirit.* New York, NY: Henry Holt and Company, 1998.

Ladendorf, Sandra F. *Successful Southern Gardening: A Practical Guide for Year-Round Beauty.* Chapel Hill, NC: University of North Carolina Press, 1989.

Lawrence, Elizabeth. *The Little Bulbs: A Tale of Two Gardens.* Durham, NC: Duke University Press, 1986.

Lawrence, Elizabeth. *A Southern Garden.* Chapel Hill, NC: University of North Carolina Press, 1943.

Lawrence, Elizabeth, and Bill Neal. *Through the Garden Gate.* Chapel Hill, NC: University of North Carolina Press, 1990.

Lipp, Lewis F., ed. *Handbook on Propagation: Propagation by Seeds, Layering, Cuttings, Grafting and Budding, Using Hormones, Mist, Plastic Film.* 2nd ed. Vol. 13. #24. Brooklyn, NY: Brooklyn Botanic Garden, 1982.

Macoboy, Stirling, and Paul Jones. *The Colour Dictionary of Camellias.* London, UK: Lansdowne Press, 1981.

Mathew, Brian. *The Smaller Bulbs.* London, UK: Batsford, 1987.

Mauritz, Sara G. *Fearless Latin: A Gardener's Introduction to Botanical Nomenclature.* CreateSpace Independent Publishing Platform, 2011.

McGourty, Frederick. *The Perennial Gardener.* Boston, MA: Houghton Mifflin, 1989.

Mellichamp, Larry, and Will Stuart. *Native Plants of the Southeast: A Comprehensive Guide to the Best 460 Species for the Garden.* Portland, OR: Timber Press, 2014.

Midgley, Jan W. *Southeastern Wildflowers.* Birmingham, AL: Crane Hill Publishers, 1999.

Mitchell, Henry. *The Essential Earthman: Henry Mitchell on Gardening.* Bloomington: Indiana University Press, 2003.

Montgomery, Betty, and Dick Carr. *A Four-Season Southern Garden.* Spartanburg, SC: James-Richards, 2013.

Ockenga, Starr. *Earth on Her Hands: The American Woman in Her Garden.* New York, NY: Clarkson Potter, 1998.

Odenwald, Neil G., and James R. Turner. *Plants for the South: A Guide for Landscape Design.* Baton Rouge, LA: Claitor's Pub. Division, 1980.

Odenwald, Neil G., and William C. Welch. *The Bountiful Flower Garden: Growing and Sharing Cut Flowers in the South.* Dallas, TX: Taylor Publishing Co., 2000.

Ogden, Scott. *Garden Bulbs for the South.* 2nd ed. Portland, OR: Timber Press, 2007.

Overy, Angela. *Sex in Your Garden.* Golden, CO: Fulcrum Publishing, 1997.

Page, Russell. *The Education of a Gardener.* New York, NY: Random House, 1983.

Phillips, Harry R., and Dorothy S. Wilbur. *Growing and Propagating Wild Flowers.* Edited by C. Ritchie Bell and Kenneth Moore. Chapel Hill, NC: University of North Carolina Press, 1985.

Poor, Janet. *Plants That Merit Attention: Trees. Vol I.* Portland, OR: Timber Press, 1984.

Poor, Janet, and Nancy Brewster. *Plants That Merit Attention: Shrubs. Vol II.* Portland, OR: Timber Press, 1984.

Pope, Alexander. *Moral Essays.* Atlanta, GA: Kudzu House, 2005.

Radford, Albert E., Harry E. Ahles, and C. Ritchie Bell. *Manual of the Vascular Flora of the Carolinas.* Chapel Hill, NC: University of North Carolina Press, 1964.

Salisbury, The Dowager Marchioness of. *A Gardener's Life.* London, UK: Frances Lincoln, 2007.

Scott, Jane. *Botany in the Field: An Introduction to Plant Communities for the Amateur Naturalist.* New York, NY: Prentice Hall Press, 1986.

Spurr, Joy, ed. *Cuttings Through the Year.* 3rd ed. Seattle, WA: University of Washington Arboretum Foundation, 2003.

Tallamy, Douglas W. *Bringing Nature Home: How Native Plants Sustain Wildlife in Our Gardens.* Portland, OR: Timber Press, 2007.

Tallamy, Douglas W., and Frederick Darke. *The Living Landscape: Designing for Beauty and Biodiversity in the Home Garden.* Portland, OR: Timber Press, 2014.

Thoreau, Henry David. *Excursions.* London, UK: Dodo Press, 2005.

Verey, Rosemary. *The Art of Planting.* Boston, MA: Little, Brown, 1990.

Verey, Rosemary. *The Garden in Winter.* Portland, OR: Timber Press, 1988.

Verey, Rosemary. *Rosemary Verey's Making of a Garden.* London, UK: Francis Lincoln, 2001.

Wasowski, Sally. *Gardening with Native Plants of the South.* Dallas, TX: Taylor Publishing, 1994.

Wells, James S. *Modern Miniature Daffodils: Species and Hybrids.* Portland, OR: Timber Press, 1989.

White, Katharine S. *Onward and Upward in the Garden.* Edited by E. B. White. New York, NY: Farrar, Straus & Giroux, 1979.

Wilson, Edward O. *Biophilia.* Cambridge, MA: Harvard University Press, 1984.

Wyman, Donald. *Wyman's Gardening Encyclopedia.* New York, NY: Macmillan Publishing, 1977.

# GENERAL INDEX

# INDEX:
## PLANTS BY COMMON NAME

# INDEX: PLANTS BY BOTANICAL NAME